The Economics of
MACRO ISSUES

The Economics of
MACRO ISSUES

FOURTH EDITION

Roger LeRoy Miller
Institute for University Studies
Arlington, Texas

Daniel K. Benjamin
Clemson University, South Carolina
and PERC, Bozeman, Montana

Addison-Wesley

New York Boston San Francisco
London Toronto Sydney Tokyo Singapore Madrid
Mexico City Munich Paris Cape Town Hong Kong Montreal

Editor in Chief: Donna Battista
Acquisitions Editor: Noel Kamm Seibert
Editorial Assistant: Carolyn Terbush
Managing Editor: Nancy H. Fenton
Senior Production Supervisor: Kathryn Dinovo
Executive Marketing Manager: Lori DeShazo
Marketing Assistant: Justin Jacob
Permissions Project Manager: Shannon Barbe
Senior Manufacturing Buyer: Carol Melville
Senior Design Supervisor: Andrea Nix
Cover Designer: Christina Gleason
Text Designer: Joseph Sherman, Dutton & Sherman
Production Coordination: Orr Book Services
Composition: Nesbitt Graphics, Inc.

Cover images, clockwise, from top right: Feverpitch/Shutterstock; Elena
Pokrovskaya/Shutterstock; Masterfile; Masterfile

Library of Congress Cataloging-in-Publication Data

Miller, Roger LeRoy.
  The economics of macro issues / Roger LeRoy Miller, Daniel K.
Benjamin. -- 4th ed.
    p. cm.
  Includes bibliographical references and index.
  ISBN 978-0-321-59454-9
  1. Macroeconomics. I. Benjamin, Daniel K. II. Title.
  HB172.5.M53 2009
  339--dc22

                                                        2009020957

1 2 3 4 5 6 7 8 9 10—CRW—13 12 11 10 09

Addison-Wesley
is an imprint of

PEARSON
www.pearsonhighered.com

ISBN-10: 0-321-59454-1
ISBN-13: 978-0-321-59454-9

CONTENTS

Part Three

Fiscal Policy

Part Four

Monetary Policy and Financial Institutions

PART FIVE

Globalization and International Finance

Suggestions for Use

At the request of our readers, we include the following table to help you incorporate the chapters of this book into your syllabus. Depending on the breadth of your course, you may also want to consult the companion paperback, *The Economics of Public Issues*, 16th edition, which features microeconomics topics and a similar table in its preface.

Economics Topics	Recommended Chapters in The Economics of Macro Issues, 4th Edition
The Recession of 2007–2009	7, 8, 11, 14, 18, 19, 24
Taxes and Public Spending	13, 14, 15, 16, 17, 18
Unemployment, Inflation, and Deflation	4, 7, 8, 11, 12
Measuring the Economy's Performance	5, 12
Economic Growth and Development	1, 2, 3, 4, 5, 10
Classical and Keynesian Macro Analyses	7, 15, 16, 18
Fiscal Policy	13, 14, 15, 16, 17, 18
Deficits and the Public Debt	14
Money and Banking	21, 22, 23
Money Creation and Deposit Insurance	22
Monetary Policy: Domestic and International	19, 20, 21
Stabilization and the Global Economy	19, 20, 25
International Trade	25, 26, 27
International Finance	27, 28

PREFACE

Times have changed, and so has this book. In the short time since our last revision, the United States has suffered a major financial panic, the housing market has collapsed, and we have endured one of the most severe recessions of the past hundred years. The response to these events has called forth a transformation of macroeconomic policymaking. The U.S. Treasury has bailed out or bought up dozens of major financial institutions. The Federal Deposit Insurance Corporation has taken over banks and, on a massive scale, has renegotiated the terms of home mortgages with individual homeowners. And the Federal Reserve System has expanded its open-market operations to include commercial paper and home mortgages and caused the reserves of the banking system to grow at unprecedented rates, even as it has driven key interest rates to near zero.

POLICY REVOLUTION

In short, things have happened to the economy that many economists had thought impossible, and the fiscal and monetary authorities have responded with nothing short of revolutionary changes in the way they conduct policy. Because this book is about our times, these changes have induced us to transform this edition of *The Economics of Macro Issues*. Whole portions of the book have been tossed out, and we have started again from scratch. The result, we believe, is a book that addresses more critical new issues with more timeliness and, we hope, more insight than any prior edition. We also believe that we are able to showcase pivotal developments in economic affairs and policymaking in ways that no other book on the market can match.

The new issues addressed in this edition include the following:

- The Panic of '08—why financial markets melted down
- Poverty, Wealth, and Equality—are the rich becoming richer and the poor becoming poorer?
- Will It Be Inflation or Deflation?—why rising prices are more likely than falling prices
- Is It Real, or Is It Nominal?—why record-high prices aren't always what they seem

- Debts and Deficits: What's a Trillion More or Less?—why there is more than meets the eye when it comes to the public debt
- Higher Taxes Are in Your Future—why you can expect to pay higher and higher taxes in the future
- Soak the Rich—what happens when a minority foots the bill for the majority
- The Hazards of High Taxes—why higher taxes can mean lower wealth
- The Fed and Financial Panics—why the Fed was founded, and what it learned from its failures
- Credit Chaos—how Congress got us into the mortgage market mess
- Deposit Insurance and Financial Markets—economic implications of subsidized deposit insurance
- Credit-Card Crunch—how new Fed rules on credit cards may keep you from getting one
- The Value of the Dollar—why exchange rates move and the consequences for America

In addition to replacing nearly half of the book, all of the remaining chapters have been touched in one way or another by the revision. Quite simply, we have sought to provide a book that reflects in every dimension the major transformations that have taken place in the American economy over the past two years. The result, we believe, will stimulate readers in unprecedented ways.

INSTRUCTOR'S MANUAL

Every instructor will want to access the *Instructor's Manual* that accompanies *The Economics of Macro Issues*. It is available online to all adopters of the book. For each chapter, the manual provides the following:

- A synopsis that cuts to the core of the economic issues involved in the chapter.
- A concise exposition of the "behind the scenes" economic analysis on which the discussion in the text is based. In almost all cases, this exposition is supplemented with one or more diagrams that we have found to be particularly useful as teaching tools.
- Answers to the Discussion Questions posed at the end of the chapter—answers that further develop the basic economic analysis of the chapter and almost always suggest new avenues of discussion.

THE REVIEW TEAM

Of course, an undertaking such as this revision requires an enormous amount of behind-the-scenes activity, and we have been fortunate to have some of the best helpmates imaginable. The following individuals contributed considerably to this revision, offering key proposals for new topics and approaches and often e-mailing us with suggestions even as the revision was taking place. To an unprecedented extent, they played an integral role in our efforts.

Olugbenga Ajilore, University of Toledo
Joe Calhoun, Florida State University
Kent Ford, Onondaga Community College
Brian Lynch, Lake Land College
Amyaz Moledina, College of Wooster
Cyril Morong, San Antonio College
Jason Rudbeck, University of Georgia
Randall Russell, Yavapai College
John Subrick, James Madison University
Deborah Walker, Fort Lewis College

To all of these individuals, we offer our most sincere thanks. Although we were unable to do everything they wanted, we believe that each of them will be able to see the impact they had on the book.

THE PRODUCTION TEAM

Our thanks also go to the individuals involved in the hands-on production process. As usual, Sue Jasin of K&M Consulting contributed expert typing and editing and Robbie Benjamin was unstinting in her demands for clarity of thought and exposition. We also thank our editors at Pearson, Noel Seibert and Carolyn Terbush, for their encouragement and help in this project. Finally, we thank John Orr of Orr Book Services for his customary expert and rapid production job.

R.L.M.
D.K.B.

PART ONE

The Miracle of Economic Growth

CHAPTER 1

Rich Nation, Poor Nation

Why do the citizens of some nations grow rich while the inhabitants of others remain poor? Your initial answer might be "because of differences in the **natural-resource endowments** of the nations." It is true that ample endowments of energy, timber, and fertile land all help increase **wealth.** But natural resources can be only a very small part of the answer, as witnessed by many counterexamples. Switzerland and Luxembourg, for example, are nearly devoid of key natural resources, and yet decade after decade, the real income of citizens of those lands has grown rapidly, propelling them to great prosperity. Similarly, Hong Kong, which consists of but a few square miles of rock and hillside, is one of the economic miracles of modern times, while in Russia, a land amply endowed with vast quantities of virtually every important resource, most people remain mired in economic misery.

UNRAVELING THE MYSTERY OF GROWTH

A number of recent studies have begun to unravel the mystery of **economic growth.** Repeatedly, they have found that it is the fundamental political and legal **institutions** of society that are conducive to growth. Of these, political stability, secure private property rights, and legal systems based on the **rule of law** are among the most important. Such institutions encourage people to make long-term investments in improvements to land and in all forms of **physical** and **human capital.** These investments raise the **capital stock,** which in turn provides for more growth long into the future. And the cumulative effects of this growth over time eventually yield much higher **standards of living.**

Table 1–1 Differing Legal Systems

Common Law Nations	Civil Law Nations
Australia	Brazil
Canada	Egypt
India	France
Israel	Greece
New Zealand	Italy
United Kingdom	Mexico
United States	Sweden

Professor Paul Mahoney of the University of Virginia, for example, has studied the contrasting effects of different legal systems on economic growth. Many legal systems around the world today are based on one of two models: the English **common law system** and the French **civil law system.** Common law systems reflect a conscious decision in favor of a limited role for government and emphasize the importance of the judiciary in constraining the power of the executive and legislative branches of government. In contrast, civil law systems favor the creation of a strong centralized government in which the legislature and the executive branch have the power to grant preferential treatment to special interests. Table 1–1 shows a sample of common law and civil law nations.

THE IMPORTANCE OF SECURE PROPERTY RIGHTS

Mahoney finds that the security of property rights is much stronger in nations with common law systems, such as the United Kingdom and its former colonies, including the United States. In nations such as France and its former colonies, the civil law systems are much more likely to yield unpredictable changes in the rules of the game—the structure of **property and contract rights.** This, in turn, makes people reluctant to make long-term fixed investments in nations with civil law systems, a fact that ultimately slows their growth and lowers the standard of living of their citizens.

The reasoning here is simple. If the police will not help you protect your rights to a home or car, you are less likely to acquire those **assets.** Similarly, if you cannot easily enforce business or employment contracts, you are much less likely to enter into those contracts—and thus less likely to produce as many goods or services. Furthermore, if you cannot plan for the future because you don't know what the rules of the game will be ten years or perhaps even one year from now, you are far less likely to make productive long-term investments that require years to pay off. Common law systems seem to do a better job at enforcing contracts and securing property rights and thus would be expected to promote economic activity now and economic growth over time.

When Mahoney examined the economic performance of nations around the world from 1960 until the 1990s, he found that economic growth has been one-third higher in the common law nations, with their strong property rights, than it has been in civil law nations. Over the years covered by his study, the increase in the standard of living—measured by **real per capita income**—was more than 20 percent greater in common law nations than in civil law nations. If such a pattern persisted over the span of a century, it would produce a staggering 80 percent differential in terms of real per capita income in favor of nations with secure property rights.

THE IMPORTANCE OF OTHER INSTITUTIONS

The economists William Easterly and Ross Levine have taken a much broader view, both across time and across institutions, assessing the economic growth of a variety of nations since their days as colonies. These authors examine how institutions such as political stability, protection of persons and property against violence or theft, security of contracts, and freedom from regulatory burdens contribute to sustained economic growth. They find that it is key institutions such as these, rather than natural-resource endowments, that explain long-term differences in growth and thus present-day differences in levels of real income. To illustrate the powerful effect of institutions, consider the contrast between Mexico, with a real per capita income of about $12,000 today, and the United States, with a real per capita income of about $48,000. Easterly and Levine conclude that if Mexico had developed with the same political and legal institutions that the United States has enjoyed, per capita income in Mexico today would be equal to that in the United States.

THE HISTORICAL ROOTS
OF TODAY'S INSTITUTIONS

In light of the tremendous importance of institutions in determining long-term growth, Easterly and Levine go on to ask another important question: How have countries gotten the political and legal institutions they have today? The answer has to do with disease, of all things. The seventy-two countries Easterly and Levine examined are all former European colonies in which a variety of colonial strategies were pursued. In Australia, New Zealand, and North America, the colonists found geography and climate that were conducive to good health. Permanent settlement in such locations was attractive, and so the settlers created institutions to protect private property and curb the power of the state. But when Europeans arrived in Africa and South America, they encountered tropical diseases—such as malaria and yellow fever—that produced high mortality among the settlers. This discouraged permanent settlement and encouraged a mentality focused on extracting metals, cash crops, and other resources. This, in turn, provided little incentive to promote democratic institutions or stable long-term property rights systems. The differing initial institutions helped shape economic growth over the years, and their persistence continues to shape the political and legal character and the standard of living in these nations today.

No Property Rights, No Property

Recent events also illustrate that the effects of political and legal institutions can be drastically accelerated—at least in the wrong direction. When Zimbabwe won its independence from Great Britain in 1980, it was one of the most prosperous nations in Africa. Soon after taking power as Zimbabwe's first (and thus far only) president, Robert Mugabe began disassembling that nation's rule of law, tearing apart the institutions that had helped it grow rich. He reduced the security of property rights in land and eventually confiscated those rights altogether. Mugabe has also gradually taken control of the prices of most goods and services in his nation and even controls the price of its national currency, at least the price at which Zimbabweans are allowed to trade it. The Mugabe government has also confiscated large **stocks** of food and most other things of value that might be exported out of or imported into Zimbabwe. In short, anything that is produced or saved has become subject to confiscation, so the incentives to do either are—to put it mildly—reduced. As a result, between 1980 and 1996, real per capita income in Zimbabwe fell by one-third, and since 1996 it has fallen by an additional third. Eighty percent of the workforce is unemployed, investment is nonexistent, and the annual inflation rate reached *231 million percent* in 2008. Decades of labor and capital investment have been destroyed because the very institutions that made progress possible have been eliminated. It is a lesson we ignore at our peril.

FOR CRITICAL ANALYSIS

1. Consider two countries, A and B, and suppose that both have identical *physical* endowments of, say, iron ore. But in country A, any profits that are made from mining the ore are subject to confiscation by the government, while in country B, there is no such risk. How does the risk of expropriation affect the *economic* endowments of the two nations? In which nation are people richer?

2. In light of your answer to question 1, how do you explain the fact that in some countries there is widespread political support for government policies that expropriate resources from some groups for the purpose of handing them out to other groups?

3. Going to college in the United States raises average lifetime earnings by about two-thirds, given our current political and economic institutions. But suppose that ownership of the added income generated by your college education suddenly became uncertain. Specifically, suppose a law was passed in your state that enabled the governor to select 10 percent of the graduating class from all of the state's colleges and universities each year and impose a tax of up to 50 percent on the difference between the earnings of these people in their first job and the average earnings of people in the state who have only a high school education. What would happen to immigration into or out of the state? What would happen to attendance at colleges and universities within the state? If the governor were allowed to arbitrarily decide who got hit with the new tax, what would happen to campaign contributions to the governor? What would happen to the number of people "volunteering" to work in the governor's next campaign? Would your decision to invest in a college education change? Explain your responses.

CHAPTER 2

Return of the Luddites: Technophobia and Economic Growth

In March 1811, General Ned Ludd and his Army of Redressers began the attacks. The objects of their rage were factories in Nottingham, England, that were using newly installed weaving machines. The **Luddites,** as they came to be known, feared that the new machines would take away their jobs and leave them unemployed. Passage of the Frame Breaking Act (which specified the death penalty for anyone who destroyed industrial machinery) soon brought a halt to the Luddites' activities. But their spirit is resurgent today in people who see catastrophe in every new technology.

TECHNOLOGY AND WEALTH

There is no doubt that technological advances have fueled **economic growth** and thereby markedly improved the lives and lengthened the life spans of human beings. Whether we look at the wheel, which drastically reduces transportation costs, or vaccines and antibiotics, which save the lives of millions of people every year, technology has raised our **wealth.** Higher wealth, in turn, enables us to make a broader range of decisions regarding the use of a wider range of **resources.** People who are wealthy can choose to have improved health for their children or higher environmental quality, or—if they are wealthy enough—both. People who are poor must watch their offspring die of preventable childhood diseases, are powerless to improve the environmental conditions in which they live, and face the prospect of never doing anything about either outcome. It is no accident that the residents of technologically advanced nations have longer life spans; they live longer because the technology has raised their wealth and enabled them to choose more healthful diets and higher-quality health care. Likewise, it is no accident that the average life span around the world rose to sixty-seven years from thirty during the twentieth century. Longevity increased because the spread of technology raised wealth and enabled people to make life-preserving and health-enhancing choices that simply were not feasible in 1900. And note finally that higher wealth, spurred by technological advances, has enabled us to choose better outcomes everywhere in our lives, including education, environmental quality, cultural amenities, and charitable activities.

To be sure, not every technological advance has made us unambiguously better off. Nuclear weapons, for example, have threatened human survival since their invention. More recently, improved knowledge of how to refine anthrax spores was used to kill people and poses the possibility of killing still more. Nevertheless, on balance, the overwhelming impact of technological advance has been to spur economic growth and, in so doing, vastly improve the economic condition of humankind.

Despite the huge benefits created by technological advances, many people in addition to Ned Ludd's Army of Redressers have objected to the introduction of new technology. Because these objections are both persistent and loudly voiced, it is important that we examine them carefully to assess their validity.

THE FEAR OF COMPETITION

The Luddites' actions were driven by one motive, pure and simple: They were hand weavers who objected to the competition offered by the new mechanized weaving machines of the day. They perceived, quite correctly, that the new machines would reduce the **demand** for hand weavers, and so they sought to prevent this competition. But the new technology did more than compel many hand weavers to learn how to use the machines or to find employment in other pursuits. It also drastically reduced the price of textiles, enabling people to own more than one set of clothes, worn all day, every day—a "luxury" that reduced deaths from cold weather in the winter and hot weather in the summer. Moreover, the rapid spread of the textile industry helped spur the development of other technology that led to the creation of new industries, such as chemicals, which have further raised our wealth. To be sure, the hand weavers were worse off, but the gains then and later to the rest of society have been staggeringly greater.

In more recent times, the fear of competition has spurred numerous other objections to technological advances. For example, when vegetable-oil-based margarine was invented around the middle of the twentieth century, the dairy industry claimed that the new product was a threat to human health (this from the purveyors of animal-fat-based butter!) and a fraud as well because the new stuff was made to look like butter. Dairy lobbyists were successful in persuading many state legislatures to outlaw yellow margarine, forcing consumers to take home white margarine from the store and mix it with yellow food coloring in their own kitchens. The substantially lower price of the new product was enough to overcome dairy industry resistance, however, and margarine became a commercial success long before the health *benefits* of vegetable oil over animal fat became apparent.

Somewhat later in the twentieth century, the development of electronic typesetting offered competition for Linotype machines, which required skilled workers to set metal type before newspapers and books could be printed. The first of these electronic typesetters, called the Photon, was four times as fast as the Linotype and could be operated by lower-wage clerical workers rather than by expensive members of the International Typographical Union (ITU). The competitive threat posed by the Photon led the ITU to call a four-month strike against all New York City newspapers in 1962–1963. The strike ended the life of the *New York Mirror,* but the remaining newspapers won from the union the right to use the Photon—in return for guaranteeing all existing ITU typesetters lifetime employment contracts. The new machines drastically reduced the costs of printing newspapers, books, and other materials, thereby raising society's wealth. Within a few decades, of course, the Photons themselves were made obsolete by yet another technological advance, the relatively low-cost but high-powered personal computer—a development no doubt objected to by Photon operators.

THE FEAR OF ADVERSE EFFECTS

It has become commonplace in recent years to object to specific new technology on the grounds that it has or *might have* adverse effects on human, animal, or plant life. This, for example, is the source of objections to irradiated food and to genetically modified food.

Fear of adverse effects stems largely from scares over DDT and other pesticides, which arose during the 1960s. It was asserted, for example, that DDT caused cancer in humans and should be banned. Despite the claims of dangers to humans, the World Health Organization has found that "the only confirmed cases of injury have been the result of massive accidental or suicidal ingestion." Moreover, the use of DDT was enormously successful in wiping out malaria in many nations around the world, saving the lives of millions of people. DDT even significantly cut the costs of raising fruits and vegetables, thereby increasing the consumption of these important cancer-fighting foodstuffs. Despite the evidence, however, most countries have banned DDT. The result has been a resurgence of malaria, the deaths of millions of people living in tropical climates, and an unequivocal threat to the lives of hundreds of millions of other human beings.

On the other side of the coin, there is evidence that indiscriminate use of DDT threatened the health and existence of numerous animal species, including the bald eagle. It is perhaps instructive, though, that recent research reveals that this harm to animal life resulted from excessive applications of DDT, that government agencies (rather than farmers) were responsible for almost all such applications, and that if the government agencies had followed the manufacturers' instructions, it is likely that no animal species would ever have been threatened.

The Fear of Wealth

Strange as it may seem, the third objection to technological advances is that they stimulate economic growth and make us richer! There are two complaints here. First, there is the argument that economic growth promotes population growth, which will eventually overwhelm our supposedly fixed resource base and thereby lead to widespread starvation and misery. Second, there is the claim that economic growth inevitably leads to environmental degradation, which in turn threatens the existence not just of humans but of all species. Whatever the plausibility of these arguments to some people, the evidence clearly refutes these notions.

Technological advances that raise our wealth *do* tend to promote population growth. After all, it takes resources to live. But the positive effect of wealth on population is much less than you might think because as people get richer, they generally have fewer children per family. Instead of pouring resources into a larger number of children, they put those resources into a higher-quality experience for the fewer children that they do rear—for example, by spending more funds on education. More important, a crucial way that technological advances raise our wealth is by enabling us to extract resources more effectively and to use those resources more efficiently. Just consider some seemingly mundane examples:

- Steam injection wells permit more complete extraction of petroleum.
- Improved machinery and designs have cut the weight of aluminum beverage cans by 40 percent.
- Advances in chemistry have created stronger, lighter plastics and longer-lasting paints and finishes.

As the result of these and thousands of other inventions, the world's reserves of oil, natural gas, aluminum, zinc, and many other commodities have *risen* over time, despite our continued use of these resources. So to be concerned that growing prosperity will cause population growth that outstrips our resources is to fail to understand the sources of that growing prosperity.

But what impact does higher wealth have on the environment? After all, more consumption necessitates more production, and that, it seems, must lead to more pollution. This reasoning would be correct if it did not ignore two crucial facts. Technological advances do help promote production, but they make it possible to produce goods with fewer inputs per unit of output, and they also make possible the development of cleaner processes, such as hybrid cars and solar power. Moreover, although early stages of economic development are often accompanied by environmental degradation, the effect is soon overwhelmed by another one. Environmental quality is a **normal good,** that is, a good that people want to consume more of as they get richer. The result is that soon after technological advances begin pushing up incomes, people begin insisting that more and more resources be devoted to protecting and enhancing environmental amenities. Indeed, once **per capita income** reaches about $8,000 in a country, environmental quality begins improving dramatically, and incomes rise even more. Thus technological advances don't merely bring us lighter beverage cans; they ultimately bring us a better environment.

THE BOTTOM LINE

The lesson of history—emphatically and unmistakably—is that technological change raises our wealth and improves the lot of humankind. Yes, there is always the *possibility* that some new technology could cause more harm than good. But what is certain is that systematic attempts to suppress technological change *almost always* cause more harm than good. It is sensible to consider carefully the potential adverse effects of new technologies and to make sure that all of the costs of those technologies are taken into account. But it is foolhardy—and impoverishing—to let unfounded fears blind us to the benefits of those technologies.

FOR CRITICAL ANALYSIS

1. If we want to obtain the maximum possible good for humankind, why is it important to take into account both the benefits and the costs of new technology, rather than simply focusing on one or the other?

2. Some people argue that a special government agency should assess, pass judgment on, and either permit or prevent the introduction of all new technological advances. Are there any reasons to think a government agency would do a better job at this (that is, benefit humankind more) than the private-sector inventors of those technologies? Are there any reasons to think such a government agency would do an inferior job?

3. Analyze the economic consequences of outlawing the wheel, which was, at the time, a major technological innovation. First, select some specific markets, and see how making the wheel illegal would affect demand and **supply** and affect the economic well-being of producers and consumers in those markets. Second, consider the economy as a whole: Is the level of real income likely to be higher or lower as a result of abolishing the wheel? How does the wheel differ from other major technological innovations, past or present?

CHAPTER 3

The Lion, the Dragon, and the Tigers: Economic Growth in Asia

In the 1980s, a group of economies in Asia came to be known as the "Asian tigers" because of their aggressive approach to **economic growth.** Among the tigers were Singapore, Malaysia, Thailand, and Indonesia. All took the view that a combination of low wages and high export sales represented the fast track to economic growth and prosperity. Now these tigers have been overtaken by the "dragon" of Asia, China—which is following the same path with perhaps even greater success.

THE GUANGDONG EXPERIMENT

For decades after the Communists' rise to power in 1949, China was best known for poverty and repression, and its aggression came mostly on the military front. But in recent years, *economic* aggression has become the Chinese byword. Although both poverty and repression are still the norm, both are changing for the better. China, it seems, is trying to learn from capitalism, even if not converting to it.

China's economic offensive began thirty years ago in its southeastern province of Guangdong. The Chinese leadership decided to use this province as a test case to see if capitalist **direct foreign investment** could stimulate economic growth in a way that could be politically controlled. The experience was deemed a success—economic growth soared amid political stability. What the government learned from the experience helped it smooth the 1997 transition of Hong Kong from British to Chinese control. Most important in terms of China's long-term economic aspirations, many foreign investors came to view the Guangdong experiment as solid evidence that they could invest in China without fear that the Communist government would confiscate their capital. Around 1992, foreign investment began to flow into China. Today, the annual rate of such investment is more than twenty times greater than it was at the beginning of the 1990s.

THAT SAME OLD SONG: DEMAND AND SUPPLY

Economic investment is being attracted to China by two powerful forces: **demand** and **supply.** On the demand side, 1.3 billion people live there, some 20 percent of the world's population. Although **per capita income** is still low by world standards, it has been growing by about 7 percent per year, after adjusting for inflation. At that rate, the **standard of living** for the Chinese people—and hence their **purchasing power** in world markets—is doubling every decade. China is already the world's largest cell-phone market, with 500 million customers. It is estimated that within a few years, China will account for 25 percent of the world's purchases of personal computers. Indeed, China now spends over $100 billion a year on information technology and services, and this amount is growing at an annual rate of 20 percent. Within two decades, the Chinese economy will likely surpass the U.S. economy and become the world's largest.

With its population of 1.3 billion individuals, China also offers attractions on the supply side. Highly skilled workers have been plentiful in the Chinese labor market. China's universities produce hundreds of thousands of engineering graduates each year. The fact that the Chinese workforce is generally well educated and often English-speaking has helped make the country attractive to foreign employers. Collaborative scientific ventures between Chinese researchers and U.S. firms are becoming increasingly common. A research team at Beijing University played a role in deciphering the genetic makeup of rice, for example. The American computer hardware and software firms Intel, IBM, Oracle, and Microsoft have shifted some key components of their research to China in recent years. Indeed, American firms of all types are setting up operations in China.

WORRIED TIGERS

Malaysia, Thailand, and Singapore are increasingly concerned by the competition they face from their neighbor to the north. Chinese medium- and high-tech industries have cut into the market share of the very sectors that helped fuel the growth of the Asian tigers. The situation is even more critical in Japan: Wages are much higher there than in China, but the Japanese technological lead over China is gradually eroding. "Are we to become a vassal of the Chinese dynasty again?" asked one Japanese official, clearly concerned that his nation's manufacturers were having trouble competing with Chinese firms. Eventually, Japan and China's other neighbors will adjust to the growing economic presence of China, but the transition may not be pleasant.

THE IMPORTANCE OF LABOR

Most observers agree that labor market developments will play a key role in the future. To this point, an important element of China's competitiveness in world markets has been the low wages there. Even though American and European firms operating in China choose to pay their workers more than state-owned enterprises pay, the firms still enjoy considerable savings. Only a few years ago, unskilled and semiskilled labor in China cost only 25 percent as much as in Europe. Moreover, in the past, foreign firms were able to hire engineers for salaries that were only 10 to 20 percent of the cost of hiring engineers in America or Europe.

Labor markets in China are changing rapidly, however. Between 2000 and 2008, average wages rose 50 percent, with bigger increases among higher-skilled workers. Many firms were unable to hire as many workers as they would have liked, and most had to upgrade their fringe benefits and other on-the-job amenities just to retain existing workers. Wages are still well below American and European levels, but the gap has closed, undercutting the competitive advantage of many Chinese firms. The most recent worldwide recession has altered labor market conditions as significantly in China as anywhere, but it is unlikely to permanently impede China's march to economic superpower status.

THE AWAKENING LION

Just to China's southwest, another giant is stirring. Around 1990, the lion of India began to throw off the self-imposed shackles of nearly a half-century of markets largely closed to international competition. The central government began opening many state-owned companies to competition from private-sector rivals. FedEx and United Parcel Service (UPS) have made huge inroads on the Indian postal service, and numerous foreign firms are now competing with the state-owned telephone service, which had long been a complete **monopoly.**

Entry into the Indian market brought familiarity with its workforce, many of whose members are fluent in English. The technical capabilities of graduates of top Indian universities, combined with their English skills and low wages, made them perfect staffers for a proliferation of call centers that have opened up across India. Tens of thousands of technical and customer-relations jobs that used to go to Middle America are now held by the growing middle class in India.

But India, too, has struggled with growth. The talent pool at the top is thin: Only a dozen or so of India's seventeen thousand universities and colleges can compete with America's best, and the wages of graduates of these top schools have soared. Moreover, India suffers from overwhelming infrastructure problems: Much of its road system is either overcrowded or in disrepair, and its port facilities are in desperate need of modernization. For the time being, such transportation problems are likely to keep India from becoming a major manufacturing powerhouse. India has also been hampered by its huge and seemingly permanent government bureaucracy. For example, despite the fact that the postal service there has lost more than half of its business to newcomers such as FedEx and UPS, none of the 550,000 postal service employees can be fired.

What Does the Future Hold?

At least India is a democracy, and its legal system, inherited from the British, who ruled there for so long, is in close conformity with the legal systems of most developed nations. Matters are rather different in China. As you saw in Chapter 1, "Rich Nation, Poor Nation," political and legal **institutions** are crucial foundations for sustained economic growth. Despite China's advances over the past thirty years, its future may be clouded unless it can successfully deal with two crucial institutional issues.

First, there is the matter of resolving the tension inherent when a Communist dictatorship tries to use capitalism as the engine of economic growth. Capitalism thrives best in an environment of freedom and itself creates an awareness of and appreciation for the benefits of that freedom. Yet freedom is antithetical to the ideological and political tenets of the Communist government of China. Will the government be tempted to confiscate the fruits of capitalist success to support itself? Or will growing pressure for more political freedom force the government to repress the capitalist system to protect itself? Either route would likely bring long-term economic growth to a halt.

The second potential problem involves China's cultural attitude toward intellectual property. In a land where imitation is viewed as the sincerest form of flattery, people routinely use the ideas of others in their own pursuits. As a result, patent and copyright laws in China are far weaker than in Western nations. Moreover, actions elsewhere considered to be commercial theft (such as software piracy) are largely tolerated in China. If foreign firms find that they cannot protect their economic **assets** in the Chinese market, foreign investment will suffer accordingly, and so will the growing dragon that depends on it so heavily.

FOR CRITICAL ANALYSIS

1. Currently, AIDS is spreading in China and India. If the governments of these nations fail to stop the spread of AIDS, what are the likely consequences for future economic growth in China and India?

2. In 1989, a massive protest against political repression in China was halted by the government's massacre of more than 150 individuals at Tiananmen Square in Beijing. What impact do you think that episode had on foreign investment and growth in China during the years immediately thereafter?

3. Presumably, the residents of China are consumers of goods as well as producers of them. Hence as growth takes place in China, not only will the worldwide supply of some goods increase, but so will the worldwide demand for other goods. What impact will Chinese economic growth have on the prices of the goods it supplies on world markets, relative to the goods it demands on world markets? Do *all* producers of goods in foreign nations lose as a result of Chinese economic growth? Do *all* consumers in foreign nations gain as a result of China's economic growth?

4. Explain how each of the following factors will influence India's ability to succeed in a highly competitive, rapidly changing global marketplace: (a) an educational system that is largely state-operated and that emphasizes job security for teachers and professors; (b) a transportation infrastructure that is largely antiquated and in disrepair; and (c) a political system that is adept at protecting favored constituents from competition and handing out favors that have concentrated benefits and widely dispersed costs.

CHAPTER 4

Outsourcing and Economic Growth

One prominent business commentator keeps a "hit list" of corporations that send jobs overseas. Such actions are decidedly un-American, he opines, whenever he gets a chance to express his views against **outsourcing.** A recent Democratic presidential nominee had a name for heads of companies that outsourced telemarketing projects, customer services, and other white-collar jobs to foreign countries: He called them "Benedict Arnold CEOs."

Congress even tried to pass a bill to prevent any type of outsourcing by the Department of State and the Department of Defense. Republican representative Don Manzullo of Illinois said, "You can't just continue to outsource overseas time after time after time, lose your strategic military base, and then expect this Congress to sit back and see the jobs lost and do nothing." When an adviser to the president publicly stated that the foreign outsourcing of service jobs was not such a bad idea, numerous politicians lambasted him for even the suggestion that outsourcing could be viewed in a positive light.

WHAT IS THIS "OUTSOURCING"?

The concept of outsourcing is simple: Instead of hiring American workers at home, American corporations hire foreign workers to do the same jobs. For example, some of these foreign workers are in India and do call-center work, answering technical questions for computer purchasers. Another job such workers do well (and cheaply) is software development and debugging. Because of low-cost communication, especially over the Internet, software programmers can be just about anywhere in the world and still work for U.S. corporations.

Besides the fear that outsourcing "robs Americans of jobs," it is also claimed that outsourcing reduces **economic growth** in the United States. (Presumably, that must mean that it increases economic growth in, say, India.) Because outsourcing is part and parcel of international trade in goods and services, the real question becomes, can the United States have higher growth rates if it restricts American corporations from "sending jobs abroad"?

As we set out to answer this question, we must keep one simple fact in mind: Outsourcing is nothing more or less than the purchase of labor services from the residents of a foreign nation. When the Detroit Red Wings host the Vancouver Canucks, fans at the game are outsourcing: They are purchasing labor services from Canadians. In this sense, Canadian hockey players are no different from Indian software engineers; they are citizens of foreign nations who are competing with citizens of the United States in the supply of labor services. Just as important, outsourcing is no different from any other form of international trade.

THE LINK BETWEEN ECONOMIC GROWTH AND OUTSOURCING

International trade has been around for thousands of years. That means that the concept of outsourcing is certainly not new, even though the term seems to be. After all, the exchange of services between countries is a part of international trade. In any event, if we decide to restrict this type of international trade in services, we will be restricting international trade in general. Experts who study economic growth today have found that the openness of an economy is a key determinant of its rate of economic growth. Any restriction on outsourcing is a type of **trade barrier,** one that will reduce the benefits we obtain from international trade.

There is a clear historical link between economic growth and trade barriers. Figure 4–1 shows the relationship between the openness of an economy—fewer or more trade barriers—and the rate of economic growth. At the bottom of the graph is a trade barrier index, which for the United States is equal to 100. On the vertical axis, you see the average annual growth of **per capita income** in percentage terms.

It is evident from this graph that countries that have fewer international trade barriers have also had higher rates of economic growth. The lesson of history is quite clear: International trade increases economic growth, and growth boosts economic well-being. Government efforts to restrict outsourcing will restrict international trade, and this will make Americans poorer, not richer.

Figure 4–1 Relationship between Economic Growth and Barriers to
International Trade

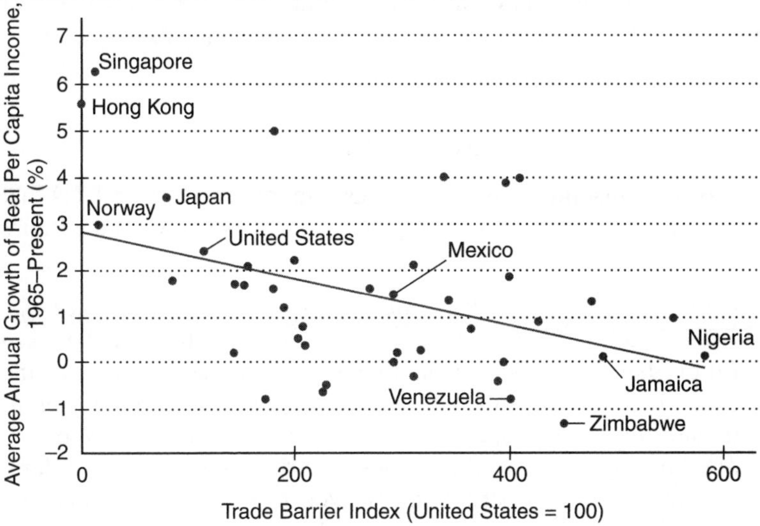

WILL THE UNITED STATES BECOME A THIRD WORLD COUNTRY?

In spite of the evidence just shown, Paul Craig Roberts, a former Reagan administration treasury official, declared at a Brookings Institution conference that "the United States will be a Third World country in twenty years." His prediction was based on the idea that entire classes of high-wage service-sector employees will eventually find themselves in competition with highly skilled workers abroad who earn much less than their U.S. counterparts. He contended that U.S. software programmers and radiologists, for example, will not be able to compete in the global economy. Thus, he argued, the United States will lose millions of white-collar jobs due to outsourcing of service-sector employment to India and China.

Jeffrey E. Garten, former dean of the Yale School of Management, reiterated and expanded on this prediction. He believes that the transfer of jobs abroad will accelerate for generations to come. He argues that in countries from China to the Czech Republic, there is a "virtually unlimited supply of industrious and educated labor working at a fraction of U.S. wages." Similarly, according to Craig Barrett, board chair at the chip maker Intel, American workers today face the prospect of "300 million well-educated people in India, China, and Russia who can do effectively any job that can be done" in the United States.

Still other commentators have claimed that India alone will soak up 3 to 4 million jobs from the U.S. labor market by 2015. Some even believe that this number may exceed 10 million. If true, one might expect American software developers and call-center technicians to start moving to India!

SOME OVERLOOKED FACTS

Much of the outsourcing discussion has ignored two simple facts that turn out to be important if we really want to understand what the future will bring.

1. *Outsourcing is the result of trade liberalization in foreign nations.* After decades of isolation, the markets in China, India, and eastern Europe have begun to open up to international trade. As is often the case when governments finally allow their people to trade internationally, these governments have pushed hard to stimulate exports— of labor services as well as goods. But this cannot be a long-term equilibrium strategy because the workers producing those goods and supplying those services are doing it because they want to become consumers. Soon enough, and this is already happening, they want to spend their hard-earned income on goods and services, many of which are produced abroad. Thus today's outsourcing of jobs to those nations must eventually turn into exports of goods and services to those same nations.

2. *Prices adjust to keep markets in balance.* The supply curve of labor is upward-sloping. Thus as U.S. corporations hire foreign workers (either directly by outsourcing or indirectly by importing goods), market wages in foreign lands must rise. Between 2003 and 2008, for example, Indian labor-outsourcing companies saw wages rise more than 40 percent. Over a longer span, real wages in southern China (which has been open to trade far longer than India) are now *six times higher* than they were just twenty years ago. These higher wages obviously reduce the competitiveness of the firms that must pay them. Moreover, it is not just wages that adjust: The relative values of national currencies move, too. Between 2003 and 2007, the value of the dollar fell more than 25 percent, making foreign goods (and workers) more expensive here and making U.S. goods and workers more attractive in foreign markets.

Of course, adjustments are never instantaneous. Moreover, they are occurring because some American firms are moving output and employment abroad; hence at least some U.S. workers are having to move to lower-paying jobs, often with a spell of unemployment along the way. How big is the impact in the short run, before all of the price adjustments take place? According to the Bureau of Labor Statistics, in a typical recent year, the number of jobs lost to outsourcing is measured in the thousands—out of a workforce of over 150 million. So if you are currently a U.S. software developer, you don't have to worry about packing your bags for Mumbai, at least not soon.

INSOURCING BY FOREIGN FIRMS

U.S. firms are not the only ones that engage in outsourcing. Many foreign firms do the same. When a foreign firm outsources to the United States, we can call it **insourcing.** For example, Mexican firms routinely send data to U.S. accounting businesses for calculation of payrolls and for maintaining financial records. Many foreign hospitals pay our radiologists to read X-rays and MRI images. Foreign firms use American firms to provide a host of other services, many of which involve consulting. Also, when a foreign automobile manufacturer builds an assembly plant in the United States, it is in effect outsourcing automobile assembly to American workers. Thus American workers in the South Carolina BMW plant, the Alabama Mercedes-Benz plant, or the Toyota or Honda plants in Tennessee and Ohio are all beneficiaries of the fact that those foreign companies have outsourced jobs to the United States. Indeed, all across the country and around the world, hundreds of millions of workers are employed by "foreign" corporations—although it's becoming difficult to tell the nationality of any company, given the far-flung nature of today's global enterprises.

WHAT REALLY MATTERS: THE LONG RUN

If you own the only grocery store in your small town, you are clearly harmed if a competing store opens across the street. If you work in a small telephone-equipment store and a large company starts taking away business via Internet sales, you will obviously be worse off. If you used to be employed at a call center for customer service at Wal-Mart and have just lost your job because Wal-Mart outsourced to a cheaper Indian firm, you will have to look for a new job.

These kinds of "losses" of income or jobs have occurred since the beginning of commerce. They will always exist in any dynamic economy. Indeed, if we look over the American economy as a whole, in a typical year roughly *one million workers lose their jobs every week*. But slightly *more* than one million people find a new job every week. So on balance, employment in the United States keeps growing, even though the average person will change jobs every three years—some, no doubt, because of international competition. But job turnover like this is an essential component of a labor market that is continually adjusting to economic change. It is a sign of health, not sickness, in the economy. If you find this hard to believe, you can look west or east. In Japan, efforts to "protect" workers from international trade resulted in economic stagnation and depressed real income growth from 1989 to 2006. In Europe, similar efforts to "preserve" the jobs of existing workers have resulted in *higher,* not lower, unemployment because firms are unwilling to hire people that they cannot fire later.

It is true that the pattern of job losses and gains in a given year are altered during an economic recession, such as the latest one. In particular, during the early stages of a recession, additional people lose their jobs in a given week and fewer people find a job each week, with the result being higher unemployment in the short run. But international trade is not the cause of recessions in the United States (although an economic recession can be made worse by *restrictions* on international trade, as it was in the early 1930s). On the contrary, international trade is an important source of economic prosperity.

If you are still wondering, simply look back at Figure 4–1. The lessons of history and of economics are clear: Trade creates **wealth,** and that is true whether the trade is interpersonal, interstate, or international. The reality is that labor outsourcing is simply part of a worldwide trend toward increased international trade in both goods and services. As international trade expands—assuming that politicians and bureaucrats allow it to expand—the result will be higher rates of growth and higher levels of income in America and elsewhere. American workers will continue to enjoy the fruits of that growth, just as they always have.

FOR CRITICAL ANALYSIS

1. What, if any, differences exist between competition among service workers across the fifty states and competition among service workers across nations?

2. When BMW decides to build a plant in the United States, who gains and who loses?

3. International Business Machines Corporation (IBM) recently stated that it expected to save almost $170 million annually by shifting several thousand high-paying programming jobs overseas. Explain why IBM would undertake this move. Then explain the short-run and long-run effects of this outsourcing.

CHAPTER 5

Poverty, Capitalism, and Growth

Fifty years ago, nearly half of the world's population lived in poverty; today, the proportion is about 17 percent. In fact, compared to fifty years ago, even though the world's population has doubled, there are actually fewer people now living below the poverty line. Despite the human misery that is evident to varying degrees in virtually every nation of the world, there is little doubt that economic prosperity has made great strides.

THE SWEEP OF HISTORY

The past half-century is but a small part of a story that has evolved over the course of 250 years. In the middle of the eighteenth century, perhaps 90 percent of the world's population lived in a state of **abject poverty,** subsisting on the equivalent of less than $1 per person per day, measured in today's terms. In fact, for most of human history, abject poverty—including inadequate nutrition and rudimentary shelter—was the norm for almost everyone, everywhere. This began to change in the eighteenth century with the **Industrial Revolution** and its associated mechanization of tasks that had always been laboriously done by humans or animals. Stimulated in the early years by the invention and application of the steam engine, the Industrial Revolution initiated a massive cascade of innovations in transportation, chemistry, biology, manufacturing processes, communications, and electronic technology. This continuing process of invention and innovation has made little headway in many parts of the world, but where it has taken hold, there has been a sustained rise in average **real per capita income** and a corresponding decline in poverty. By 1820, the extent of abject poverty had fallen from 90 percent to 80 percent; by 1900, it had dipped below 70 percent; and it has continued to decline since. Before the Industrial Revolution, more than five out of six people lived in abject poverty; today, it is one out of six.

Uneven Progress

This story of human progress has been uneven across countries. Europe, North America, and a few other locations have witnessed the greatest increases in real per capita income and the greatest decreases in poverty. By contrast, the **standard of living** and the extent of poverty in most nations in Africa have changed little over the past 250 years. Even within given countries, progress has sometimes been erratic. Ninety years ago, for example, the standard of living in Argentina was the sixth highest in the world; today, that nation ranks seventieth in living standards. In contrast, thirty years ago, 250 million people in China lived in abject poverty; that number has since been cut to one-tenth that number.

In Chapter 1, "Rich Nation, Poor Nation," you saw the key institutional factors that determine average levels of **per capita income.** Secure **property and contract rights** and the **rule of law** were the **institutions** under which the Industrial Revolution flourished best, and it is thus in nations that have embraced these institutions that people are most likely to be prosperous. These same institutions are the ones typically associated with *capitalism,* economic systems that depend primarily (though not necessarily completely) on markets to allocate scarce **resources.** Of course, no country in the world is completely capitalist; in the United States, for example, less than two-thirds of resources are allocated by the private sector, while the rest are allocated by federal, state, or local governments. At the other end of the spectrum, even in Communist countries such as Cuba, Vietnam, and North Korea, markets play at least some role in allocating resources.

Despite a few ambiguities, then, it is possible to measure the degree of capitalism (or, as some would term it, economic freedom) in each country around the world. Doing so yields measures that seem to correspond reasonably well with what many people would think is true about the economies of those countries. For example, using the measures constructed by Canada's Fraser Institute, Hong Kong's economy is rated the most capitalist, while the United States is tied for third (with Switzerland and New Zealand). Singapore, Canada, Ireland, and Australia are other nations whose economies are judged among the ten most capitalist in the world. If you know much about economic prosperity around the world, you will be aware that these countries are also among the world leaders in real per capita income. Indeed, the association of capitalism with prosperity is everywhere quite strong.

CAPITALISM AND PROSPERITY

It is convenient for our purposes to divide all the nations in the world into five groups, ranging from "most capitalist" to "least capitalist." Data limitations prevent doing this with every single nation. Nevertheless, it is possible to do it for about 125 of them, putting 25 nations into each of the five groups. Thus among the top 25 "most capitalist" nations, in addition to the countries we mentioned earlier, many (but not all!) of the original members of the **European Union (EU)** would be included, along with Chile, Costa Rica, and Kuwait. At the other end of the spectrum, the economies of Russia, Algeria, Venezuela, and Zimbabwe would all fall into the group of the 25 "least capitalist" nations.

As we suggested earlier, people who live in the most capitalist nations in the world also tend to have the highest average income. For example, average per capita income for people living in the group including the 25 most capitalist nations averages over $23,000 per year. For people living in the next most capitalist group of nations, per capita income averages about $13,000 per year. Once we get down to the 25 least capitalist nations, average income has dropped to but $3,300 per year. And because rates of economic growth are *also* higher in more capitalist nations, the differences in income between the most and least capitalist nations are growing over time.[1]

Of course, this is a chapter about poverty, and the *average* income in a nation may bear little relation to the income earned by its poorest residents. Many people believe, for example, that capitalist nations promote excessively competitive behavior so that people who are not good at competing end up much poorer in capitalist than in noncapitalist nations. If the rich get richer in capitalist countries while the poor get poorer, then even if the average person in capitalist nations is doing well, the same might not be true for people at the bottom of the income distribution. As it turns out, however, the poor do *not* do worse in capitalist countries; in fact, they do better.

CAPITALISM AND POVERTY

Consider the 25 most capitalist nations in the world. On average, the poorest 10 percent of the population receives about 2.5 percent of total income in these countries. Indeed, if we look across *all* countries, we see

---

1. All income comparisons are made using a method called **purchasing power parity (PPP),** generally acknowledged to be the most accurate means of making comparisons across nations with very different income levels and consumption bundles.

that although there is some variation from nation to nation, the poorest 10 percent of the population typically gets between 2.0 and 2.5 percent of total income. One way to put this is that on average, capitalism does *not* lower the share of total income going to the people at the bottom of the income distribution. Capitalist or Communist, in Africa or in the Americas, the per capita income of the poorest 10 percent of the population in a nation ends up being about one-quarter of what it is in the middle of the income distribution for that country.

Now if you followed the numbers earlier about average income and capitalism, you may already have figured out the next point: Because capitalism raises total income in a nation without reducing the *share* of income going to the poor, capitalism ends up raising income at *all* points in the income distribution. Thus for the poorest 10 percent of the population in highly capitalist countries, average per capita income is about $5,900 per year (or just under $24,000 per year for a family of four). For the poorest 10 percent of the population in the least capitalist countries, average income is under $750 per year (about $3,000 for a family of four). Expressed somewhat differently, poor people in the most capitalist nations can expect average income levels *eight times higher* than poor people in the least capitalist nations.

The radically better standard of living experienced by the poor in capitalist nations is reflected in many other statistics indicative of quality of life. For example, life expectancy in the 25 most capitalist nations is about seventy-seven years; in the least capitalist, it is about fifty-seven. Similarly, infant mortality rates are *eight times higher* in the least capitalist countries than in the most capitalist. Moreover, because people at the top of the income distribution have access to health care in both rich and poor nations, these differences in life expectancy and infant mortality are chiefly due to differences among people at the bottom of the income distribution. In capitalist nations, compared to noncapitalist countries, it is the poor whose newborns are surviving infancy and whose adults are surviving to old age.

There is another compelling difference between capitalist and noncapitalist countries that sheds light on what the future may bring. In the 25 most capitalist countries of the world, fewer than 1 percent of children under the age of fifteen are working rather than in school. In the 25 least capitalist nations, one child of every six under the age of fifteen is working rather than in school—a rate nearly twenty times higher. Thus in capitalist nations, children are much more likely to be getting the education necessary for them to learn the skills of the future. This in turn means that **economic growth** is likely to be higher in capitalist than in noncapitalist nations, and this is exactly what we observe. Growth in per capita income in the 25 most capitalist countries averages about 2.3 percent per year, enough to double income at all levels over the next thirty years. In contrast, average per capita incomes are actually *falling* in the least capitalist countries, implying that the misery of today's poor in these nations is likely to get worse.

More than Numbers

It is easy to get too wrapped up in numbers, so it may be useful to make a few simple head-to-head comparisons. Consider North Korea and South Korea. Both emerged from World War II with shattered economies, only to fight each other in the Korean War. When the war was over, South Korea embraced capitalism, building an economy based on the rule of law, secure property rights, and a reliance on the market as the primary means of allocating scarce resources. North Korea rejected all of these, choosing instead a Communist system that relied on centralized command and control to allocate resources—a system ruled not by law but by one man at the top. South Korea became a world economic powerhouse, with per capita income of almost $25,000 per year. North Korea stagnated and, with a per capita income of only $1,900 per year, must now rely on foreign aid to feed many of its people.

If we were to look at East Germany and West Germany between World War II and the fall of the Berlin Wall in 1989, we would see the same story repeated. West Germany embraced the central principles of a market-based capitalist economy and prospered. East Germany rejected those principles, and its people were impoverished. A similar tale of two countries can be told in comparing the economies of Taiwan and China between 1950 and 1980: Capitalist Taiwan prospered while Communist China stagnated—and people at the bottom of the income distribution suffered the most.

Indeed, as noted in Chapter 3, China itself presents us with a tale of two countries: the Communist version before 1980 and the increasingly capitalist one of the years since. After decades of post–World War II stagnation under communism, the gradual move toward market-based resource allocation in China since 1980 is transforming life for people at all levels of income. Overall, real per capita income has roughly doubled every decade since 1980. Moreover, at least in those areas of the country where the Communists have let the capitalists try their hand, this economic progress has been widespread and sustained. So even though political freedom in China is not yet to be had, the growing economic freedom in that nation is having the same impact it has had around the world and over time: When people are able to enjoy secure property rights, the rule of law, and a reliance on markets as allocators of scarce resources, people at *all* points in the distribution benefit.

FOR CRITICAL ANALYSIS

1. The income measures discussed in this chapter do not include non-cash benefits that are often available to low-income individuals, such as food stamps and Medicaid. Do you think such noncash benefits are more likely to be made available to poor people in a rich nation or in a poor nation? Explain your answer. Hint: Do people get more or less charitable as their incomes rise? Then ask yourself, how will the difference in noncash benefits in rich nations versus poor nations affect your conclusions regarding relative incomes of poor individuals in capitalist nations compared to noncapitalist nations? Explain this answer as well.

2. How would a political system in which there is the rule of law (that is, in which the same rules apply to everyone) serve to protect people at the bottom of the income distribution most strongly?

3. In light of the analysis in Chapter 1 and the information presented in this chapter, what are some ways that people in developed nations might help people in developing nations achieve higher income levels? Explain, giving specific examples, if you can.

PART TWO

The Business Cycle, Unemployment, and Inflation

CHAPTER 6

Measuring GDP

Overall business activity in any country never stays the same. There are "booms" and "busts"—**expansions** and **recessions**—even though the long-term trend may be up. Even noneconomists can agree on some of the obvious signs of an "up" in business activity (expanding corporate **profits,** higher employment, rising business investment spending) and the obvious signs of "down" periods (rising unemployment, falling profits, more idle production capacity). But the one traditional *overall* measure of business activity is being seriously questioned. This measure is **gross domestic product (GDP),** which is a measure of the total market value of final goods and services produced in a country in any one year.

Unless you have a deep and abiding love of accounting, you may be wondering, why should I read this chapter? There are two reasons. First, almost all macroeconomic policy is driven by policymakers' perceptions of what is happening to a few key variables, perhaps the most important of these being GDP. So if you want to understand the policies now in place or being contemplated, you must start by understanding how GDP is calculated and what it does and does not measure. Second, as you saw in Chapter 5, "Poverty, Capitalism, and Growth," the human condition varies dramatically around the globe. Radical differences in prosperity and poverty from one nation to the next can be understood only if we begin with a clear awareness of what is being measured. And that awareness starts with measuring GDP.

What Does GDP Measure?

The way GDP is measured has been under attack for some time. There are two separate issues here. First, does GDP measure what the U.S.

Department of Commerce *claims* it measures? For example, if someone were to produce and sell you an illegal good, the transaction has resulted in a new, domestically produced final good and should be counted in GDP as a matter of definition. But because neither you nor the producer of the good is likely to report this trade to the Department of Commerce, it is unlikely that the transaction will make it into the official statistics.

The second issue has to do with whether GDP measures *welfare* (the general level of satisfaction), which is what some people seem to think it measures. News commentators, for example, often speak of the latest GDP numbers as though they are the definitive measure of "how America is doing." But GDP is a measure of the *market value* of newly produced final goods and services. It can change when the *quantities* of those products increase or decrease or when the *prices* of those products go up or down. If the prices of goods and services change in the absence of a corresponding change in the quantity or quality of those items, GDP will change. Yet the level of satisfaction of individuals is unlikely to have changed under such circumstances. Hence this is a case where a change in GDP clearly does *not* signal a change in the level of satisfaction (or welfare) of individuals.

It is possible to adjust GDP for changes in the **price level.** Doing so results in something called **real GDP.** Whether this number is good as a measure of welfare is itself subject to debate, but at least the effects of changes in price levels have been eliminated, giving us a concrete measure of the amount of goods and services that are newly produced in the economy. In this chapter, we focus on the strengths and weaknesses of real GDP and use this term to describe what we are measuring. But be warned: Not all commentators and journalists are careful in distinguishing between *GDP* and *real GDP,* so you will have to be on the alert when you read or listen to news reports.

Accounting for Missing Information

As a general rule, to "correct" real GDP, we should *add* what is not measured but should be and *subtract* what is included but should not be. Interestingly enough, the Department of Commerce already devotes considerable effort to making sure that real GDP is as accurate as possible when it comes to measuring what it claims to measure. For example, even though there is no "market" in owner-occupied housing, the Commerce Department has devised methods of estimating the implicit rental value of houses occupied by their owners, and it includes the aggregate value of these services in its published measure of real GDP.

In a similar vein, farmers consume some of the food items they produce before those items ever get to the market. Again, the Commerce

Department has devised ways to estimate the market value of such food, using methods that take into account typical **consumption** patterns, family size, and the like. As with owner-occupied housing, these estimates are included in the official GDP numbers.

WHAT IS STILL MISSED

Despite the government's best efforts, there are some major omissions from published measures of real GDP. For example, do-it-yourself activities are not included in the official measures, even though they constitute the production of a service. If you take your car to a mechanic, the services performed on the car end up as part of measured real GDP. But if you and a friend repair your car, these services are not included in the statistics. (We need to be careful here: Any parts or tools you buy from local stores *are* included in measured real GDP. It is the labor component—the value of the time you and your friend put into the repairs—that escapes detection and thus inclusion in real GDP. And because labor typically accounts for about two-thirds of the value of output, this means that in cases such as this, more may be excluded than included.)

The biggest category of do-it-yourself services left out of the official GDP statistics consists of those performed in the house by homemakers. The value of the services performed by homemakers who are not explicitly paid can indeed be large. Every year, various sources estimate the value of these services based on the going wage rates that would have to be paid to provide the services if the homemaker did not. By now, the *weekly* value of a homemaker's services is estimated at over $800. With many millions of such individuals spread across the country, the implied undermeasurement of newly produced final goods and services is huge. We should note, however, that homemakers' services counted in real GDP have been steadily increasing over the past thirty years. This is because women have poured into the paid workforce and now purchase in the market more and more of the services that they used to perform themselves. Each time a (former) homemaker hires another individual or firm to do something, that activity will be counted in real GDP.

Then there is the matter of the huge volume of transactions—hundreds of billions of dollars per year—in markets for illegal and underground activities. In some "true" measure of real GDP, we should probably add the value of these activities, which include prostitution and the illegal drug trade, because such goods and services presumably generate satisfaction to the individuals purchasing them. We should also include "underground" income that is the result of legal activities but is not reported. Some of this income goes unreported by individuals hoping to evade income taxes. But it also includes much of the income earned by illegal immigrants, who do not report their incomes simply because they do not wish to be deported.

The final bit of "income" that we should account for, especially if we are interested in closing the gap between official income measures and the well-being of the citizenry, is the amount of time people have for leisure. After all, leisure is a good, and it is scarce. It has value and generates satisfaction. For the civilian economy, average weekly hours worked have fallen from over forty-eight in 1943 to under thirty-four in 2009, a definite increase in the real **standard of living** for the individuals enjoying this added leisure time.

SUBTRACTIONS NEEDED TOO

What about things that are newly produced but don't really belong in real GDP? The most important of these are **intermediate goods**—goods that contribute to present or future consumer welfare but are not direct sources of utility themselves. Here again, the accountants at the Department of Commerce have done much of the work for us, because most of these goods are handled in the normal construction of the real GDP figure. For example, the steel, plastic, aluminum, rubber, and other components that go into making a car end up being counted only once—in the form of the car itself. All of the earlier market transactions involving the components that make up the car are subtracted before the official figures for real GDP are published. Nevertheless, there are still some intermediate goods that *should* be deducted but are not, including such items as personal business expenses and commuting costs. For example, the government statisticians treat as equivalent the $5 you spend on gasoline to go on a date in the evening and the $5 you spend on gasoline for your trip to work in the morning.

The next category of expenditures that might be considered worthy of subtraction is sometimes referred to as "regrettable necessities." This includes spending for diplomacy, national security, police and fire protection, and prison facilities. Unlike sports cars and prom dresses, battle tanks and body armor are not produced because they yield consumer satisfaction in and of themselves. They are produced because they make it possible for us to enjoy the consumption of other goods. For example, during World War II, automobile assembly lines were converted into assembly lines used to make military vehicles that helped us win the war—and thus resume our way of life afterward. In this sense, we can think about regrettable necessities as intermediate goods that go into the production of other goods. As such, they probably should be subtracted from real GDP, but the government statisticians won't hear of it.

It is also important to recognize that the urbanized, industrialized society that makes it possible for us to have many of the goods we consume has some drawbacks. Big cities make large-scale commercial activities (and thus more market goods) feasible. But they also bring with them a variety of urban disamenities, such as congestion, noise, and litter. If we want to narrow the gap between the official statistics and some measure of welfare, we should make deductions from real GDP for such sources of dissatisfaction. It is difficult to put a precise numerical value on them, however, and so none of the official statistics are adjusted. Similar considerations apply when economic activity causes a reduction in environmental quality. Air, water, and view pollution all reduce consumer welfare, but they are sufficiently difficult to quantify that the accountants make no deductions when pollution increases and no additions when pollution control measures yield environmental improvements.

What Do We Know When?

If you have been following closely thus far, you can appreciate the fact that keeping track of GDP is a huge undertaking. There are, after all, more than 23 million businesses in the United States, producing vast numbers of goods and employing more than 140 million people. Perhaps for this reason it often takes quite a while before we really know what's going on with GDP.

The Commerce Department constructs estimates of GDP every calendar quarter (three-month period), reporting numbers as *annual rates,* that is, what GDP would be for a year if it continued at its level for that quarter. Here is where it gets interesting (or tedious, if you hate numbers). One month after the end of each quarter, the Commerce Department issues an "advance" report on GDP; a month later, it issues a "preliminary" report; and after another month, it announces its "final" estimate of GDP for that quarter. But it is not over yet: Frequently, sometimes many months later, the Commerce Department issues a "revised" estimate of GDP. And every once in a while it will go back a few years later and revise the revisions!

There are two consequences of all this estimating and revising. The first is that there is a steady stream of numbers coming out on GDP, some for the latest quarter, some for an earlier quarter, and some for quarters or years past. Unless you look at the fine print, it is sometimes hard to tell exactly what the bureaucrats are trying to tell us about the state of the economy. This brings us to our second point. As we discuss more fully in the next chapter, although measures of GDP are *not* the basis on which economic expansions and recessions are officially classified, many of the components of GDP go into the determination of whether the economy is expanding or contracting. And with all of the revisions of these numbers, it is easy to see why it gets pretty hard to pin down exactly where we are and where we might be going. Thus it was that it took fully a *year* for the number crunchers to decide that the latest recession started in December 2007 and not, say, six months before or twelve months after that date.

WHAT DOES IT ALL MEAN?

For centuries, macroeconomic policymakers have sought to understand how the economy is doing and where it is headed next. Not until the twentieth century, with the first systematic measurements of GDP, did they begin to develop such an understanding. We have seen that GDP sometimes doesn't measure what it is designed to measure, it often doesn't measure what some people think it ought to measure, and it usually doesn't measure it when we'd like it to. Most important, it is crucial when making comparisons over time or across nations to account for differences in the price level—to focus on real GDP. Even once we do this, we have seen that ambiguities and errors remain—illegal goods, underground markets, disamenities, and regrettable necessities, to name but a few. Nevertheless, for all its weaknesses, real GDP continues to be used by policymakers, reported on by journalists, and editorialized about by commentators for one simple reason: It beats all the alternatives in helping us understand how the economy is doing and where it is headed next.

FOR CRITICAL ANALYSIS

1. How does one determine what is a final good or service and what is a regrettable necessity or an intermediate good? In other words, where does one draw the line?

2. Why can't we conclude that welfare is proportional to annual national consumption?

3. Would you categorize each of the following expenditures as intermediate goods, regrettable necessities, or consumption goods: (a) a spare tire, (b) surgery to repair a badly broken arm, (c) a Botox injection to remove forehead wrinkles, (d) voice lessons, and (e) expenditures on your college education? Explain your reasoning in each case. Would your answers to (c) and (d) change if you knew that the purchaser was a professional singer who made many public appearances? Why or why not?

CHAPTER 7

What's in a Word? Plenty, When It's the "R" Word

Incumbent presidents (and members of their political party) hate the "R" word. We speak here of **recession,** a word used to describe a downturn or stagnation in overall, nationwide economic activity. Politicians' attitudes toward recessions are driven by the simple fact that people tend to "vote their pocketbooks." That is, when the economy is doing well, voters are likely to return incumbent politicians to office, but when the economy is doing poorly, voters are likely to "throw the bums out." Interestingly, although *recession* is the word most commonly used to describe a period of poor performance by the economy, most people don't really know what the word means.

THE NBER

Ever since its founding in 1920, a private organization called the National Bureau of Economic Research (NBER) has sought to accurately measure the state of overall economic conditions in the United States. (It also sponsors research on other economic issues.) Over time, the NBER developed a reputation for measuring the economy's performance in an evenhanded and useful way. As a result, most people now accept without argument what the NBER has to say about the state of the economy. And most notably, this means that it is the NBER that we rely on to tell us when we are in a recession.

If you are an avid reader of newspapers, you may well have heard a recession defined as any period in which there are at least two quarters (three-month periods) of declining **real gross domestic product (real GDP).** In fact, the NBER's recession-dating committee places little reliance on the performance of real (inflation-adjusted) GDP when deciding on the state of the economy. There are two reasons for this. First, the government measures GDP only on a quarterly basis, and the NBER prefers to focus on more timely data that are available at least monthly. Second, the official GDP numbers are subject to frequent and often substantial revisions, so what once looked like good economic performance might suddenly look bad, and vice versa.

Looking back at 2001 (a turbulent year), for example, the initial figures showed that real GDP declined in only one quarter during the year. But when the government finally finished all of its revisions to the data, it turned out that real GDP actually fell during *three* quarters of 2001. In 2007, the government issued a revision of its revised GDP figures for 2004–2006. Of the twelve quarters covered by this "revision of the revisions," the numbers for all twelve were changed: Two were revised upward and ten downward. One can easily see why an organization such as the NBER, which prides itself on reliability and accuracy, might be reluctant to place too much weight on measures of real GDP.

So what does the NBER use as its criteria in measuring a recession? Its official definition of a recession gives us some insight: "A recession is a significant decline in activity spread across the economy, lasting more than a few months, visible in industrial production, employment, real income, and wholesale-retail sales." Those are a lot of words to define just one term, but it's not too difficult to get a handle on it. The point to note at the outset is that the NBER focuses chiefly on four separate pieces of information:

- Industrial production
- Employment
- Real income (measured by inflation-adjusted personal income of consumers)
- Sales at both the wholesale and retail levels

All of these figures are reliably available on a monthly basis, and so every month, the NBER uses the latest figures on each to take the pulse of the economy. When all four are moving upward, that's generally good news. When all are moving downward, that's definitely bad news. And when some are moving in one direction and some in another direction, that's when expert judgment comes into play.

The Three *D*'s

If the NBER recession-dating committee uses a strict formula to time the onset or end of a recession, the committee members don't reveal what it is. What they do reveal is that they are looking for three crucial elements, all starting with the letter *D,* when they officially announce the start or end of a recession:

1. *Depth.* If there is a downturn in one or more of the four key variables, the NBER focuses first on the magnitude of that downturn. For example, in an economy like ours with total employment of over 140 million, a drop in employment of 50,000 would not be crucial; an employment drop of, say, one million surely would be considered significant.

2. *Duration.* Month-to-month fluctuations in economic activity are the norm in our economy. These fluctuations occur partly because our measures of economic activity are imperfect and partly because, in an economy as complex as ours, many things are happening all the time that have the capacity to affect the overall performance of the economy. Thus if real personal income moves up or down for a month or even two months in a row, the recession-dating committee is likely to determine that such a change is well within the bounds of normal variation. But if a trend persists for, say, six months, the committee is likely to place a much heavier weight on that movement.

3. *Dispersion.* Because the NBER is trying to measure the overall state of the economy, it wants to make sure it is not being misled by economic developments that may be important to many people but are not reliable indicators of the overall state of the economy. For example, America is becoming less dependent on industrial production and more reliant on service industries. In addition, it is well known that industrial production is sensitive to sharp movements not shared by sectors elsewhere in the economy. So the NBER tempers the importance of industrial production by simultaneously relying on measures such as wholesale and retail sales to make sure it has a picture of what is happening throughout the economy.

A Precise Answer

Having blended its four measures of the economy in a way that reflects its focus on the three *D*'s, the recession-dating committee makes its decision. A recession, in its view, begins "just after the economy reaches a peak of activity" and ends "as the economy reaches its trough" and starts expanding again. Between trough and peak, the economy is said to be in an **expansion.** Historically, the normal state of the economy is expansion; most recessions are brief (usually ending within twelve to eighteen months), and in recent decades, they have been rare. Our most recent recession began in December 2007 after six years of economic expansion.

The four measures used by the NBER to date recessions generally move fairly closely together. Although individually they sometimes give conflicting signals for short periods of time, they soon enough start playing the same song. Nevertheless, some contention about the NBER's decisions remains. There are two sources of debate. One focuses on *potential* growth of economic activity, and the other highlights the importance of population growth.

The NBER defines a recession as an absolute decline in economic activity. But some economists note that at least for the past couple of centuries, growth in economic activity from year to year has been the norm in most developed nations, including the United States. Hence, they argue, a recession should be declared whenever growth falls significantly below its long-term potential. This dispute becomes more important when there is reason to believe that potential growth has shifted for some reason or when comparing the current performance of two nations that are growing at different rates. For example, suppose nation X has potential growth of 4 percent per year while nation Y has potential growth of only 2 percent per year. If both are actually growing at 2 percent, the unemployment rate in X will be rising, and some people would argue that this fact is sufficient to declare that X is in a state of recession. The biggest problem with this proposed measure of recession is that it is difficult to declare with confidence exactly what the potential growth rate of any country is.

The second point of contention starts with the observation that the population is growing in most countries. Hence even if economic activity is growing, the well-being of the average citizen might not be. For example, suppose the population is growing 3 percent per year but real personal income is growing only 2 percent a year. Assuming that the other measures of activity were performing like personal income, the NBER would say the economy was in an expansion phase, even though **real per capita income** was declining. Some economists would argue that this state of affairs should be declared a recession, given that the term is supposed to indicate a less-than-healthy economy. This point has some validity. Nevertheless, there have not been many prolonged periods when the NBER has said the economy was expanding while real per capita income was falling.

Ultimately, of course, even if the recession-dating committee somehow tinkered with its methods to better acknowledge the importance of potential growth and population changes, some other issue would undoubtedly be raised to dispute the NBER's conclusions. For now, most economists are content to rely on the NBER to make the call. Most politicians are, too—except, of course, when it suits them otherwise. As for ordinary voters, well, even if they don't know how a recession is defined, they surely know what one feels like—and are likely to vote accordingly.

FOR CRITICAL ANALYSIS

1. Why is it important, both for the political process and for our understanding of the economy, for the NBER to resist the temptation to change its definition of a recession to fit the latest political pressures or economic fads?

2. Do you think that voters care more about whether the NBER says the economy is in a state of recession or whether they and their friends and family members are currently employed in good jobs? Why do politicians make a big deal over whether the economy is "officially" in a recession or an expansion? (*Hint:* Is it hard for the average voter to tell what is going on in the economy outside his or her community, leaving the voter dependent on simple measures—or labels—of what is happening elsewhere in the economy?)

3. Examine the data from the last six recessions. (Good sources for data are www.nber.org/cycles/recessions.html, www.bea.gov, and www.globalindicators.org.) Rank them on the basis of both duration and severity. The first is easy; the second is more difficult: Is it possible that some people—either politicians or other citizens—might disagree about how to measure the severity of a particular recession? How would you measure it?

CHAPTER 8

The Panic of '08

The risk is small—1 in 10,000 over a ten-year period. That is the chance that a borrower will default on the highest-grade, so-called triple A (AAA) debt according to Moody's, one of the three government-approved investment-rating agencies in the United States. Trillions of dollars of debt instruments rated AAA were floating around the world in 2008. By the end of that year, about a half a trillion dollars of that AAA-rated "paper" was in default. That meant that millions of individuals, **mutual funds, hedge funds,** banks, city governments, and state governments ended up losing hundreds of billions of dollars—and this was just on the "low-risk" **bonds.** Losses on riskier **assets** were even greater.

To understand how the United States and the world suffered the greatest financial meltdown since the 1930s, we have to go back at least fifteen years.

THE BIG FEDERAL PUSH TO EXPAND HOME OWNERSHIP

As you will see in Chapter 21, "Credit Chaos," starting in 1995, both Congress and the Clinton administration began pushing hard for banks and other mortgage-lending institutions to relax the standards applied to anyone seeking a home **mortgage.** The goal was to increase home ownership, particularly among lower-income U.S. residents.

Mortgage-lending institutions got the message. They began relaxing standards for down payments, credit histories, and other barometers of financial risk. Many of the new home loans they made were labeled subprime or Alt-A (so-called borderline mortgages). After the recession of 2001–2002, the two giant government-sponsored mortgage corporations,

Fannie Mae and Freddie Mac, began pushing lenders to offer even more mortgage loans of dubious quality. Soon almost anyone could get a mortgage, and within a short period of time, a housing boom took flight. Low- and even no-income individuals were realizing the American dream of home ownership—with lots of debt to pay back.

TAKING THE RISK OUT OF SUBPRIME MORTGAGES: MBSs, ABSs, AND CDOs

No lending institution, even the most risk-loving, would continue to make a larger and larger share of its loans to risky borrowers if it could not shift some or all of the risk elsewhere. Enter the **mortgage-backed security,** or **MBS.** Back in the 1970s, Fannie Mae and Freddie Mac had begun buying up mortgage loans and packaging them as MBSs. Every lending institution that sold its high-risk mortgages for use in MBSs reduced its risk. During the 1980s, **investment banks** got involved in MBSs. They started selling packages of MBSs throughout the world, albeit on a modest scale at that time.

Then investment banks came up with something called an **asset-backed security,** or **ABS.** First created by investment banks in the 1990s, these **investment security** "packages" really took off in 2003 when subprime mortgage loans and other risky loan assets were packaged together. Even this packaging was not enough to distribute all of the risk, so investment bankers resurrected an investment vehicle called a **collateralized debt obligation,** or **CDO.** These investment securities were created by mixing asset-backed securities, subprime loans, and other credit-related contracts all into one package.

NO DATA, NO PROBLEM

With all these new investment entities floating around, Wall Street investment bankers had a hard time assessing their respective risks. These were new financial instruments, and many purchasers simply bought and held them. The result was that the market for these assets was relatively illiquid. Lacking market-based data on risks, the investment banks relied on their programmers to create computer models of potential risk. But the programmers (often called "quants" because they constructed quantitative numerical models) had limited data on which to base the accuracy of their risk models. And what was worse, the data that they did have on subprime mortgage defaults were deceiving: Yes, it was true that during the period 2003–2005 many subprime borrowers were paying their mortgages on time. But the whiz kids of Wall Street did not realize that these subprime mortgage borrowers were paying their debts with *additional* borrowing. Borrowers' debts were growing, not shrinking, as the Wall Street quants had mistakenly thought.

So at the same time, based on fundamentally flawed assumptions, the rating agencies (such as Moody's) were bestowing triple A ratings on vast quantities of subprime-mortgage-related investment securities—hundreds of billions of dollars' worth. At the peak, 90 percent of **securitized** subprime loans had magically turned into investment securities with a top rating of AAA (or the equivalent).

THE MARKET TURNS

Many of the mortgage loans made in 2003–2005 entailed relatively low initial monthly payments that sharply escalated after two to three years. When these payments began rising on a wide scale in late 2005 and early 2006, many borrowers could not make those increased payments, and the housing **bubble** burst with a vengeance. Individuals who had purchased homes hoping to sell them for a quick **profit** found themselves "underwater," referring to the fact that the market values of their properties were suddenly less than what they owed. A lot of individuals just walked away from their mortgage debts and their houses.

All of the entities that owned MBSs, ABSs, and CDOs were suddenly receiving billions of dollars less in monthly mortgage payments. Moreover, it was clear that the market value of these securities and obligations was going to turn out to be less than people had anticipated. But how much less would it be?

MARK TO MARKET MEANT MANY MARKDOWNS

Suppose you are trying to determine how much you are worth. In one column, you write down the values of your assets—cars, houses, savings accounts, stocks, and bonds. In the other column, you add up all of your **liabilities**—mortgages, car loan outstanding, credit-card balances, and so on. When you subtract the latter from the former, you end up with your **net worth.**

Now suppose that one of your assets is a ten-year U.S. Treasury bond for which you paid $10,000 seven years ago. There are three years to go before it will mature—meaning that the federal government will pay off the bond then. If you look in the newspaper today, you might find that the market value of that ten-year bond with three years remaining is, say, $9,500. Or the market value might be $10,300. What should you do when figuring out your actual assets? Should you **mark to market,** that is, value it at current "market" value? Or should you just figure that because you are going to get your $10,000 in three years (plus interest in the intervening period), you will assess the value at $10,000? Your answer depends on the purpose for which you want the estimate of your net worth.

Among accountants, an archaic principle holds that you should mark to market, or use what is called **fair-value accounting.** In other words, you should adjust your **balance sheet** (assets and liabilities) when the market values of your financial assets or liabilities change. This seems like a harmless and sensible accounting principle. For financial institutions, it requires them to adjust their balance sheets when the market values of the financial assets that they own change. Many of those financial institutions do in fact hold ten-year Treasury bonds, as noted earlier. They also hold **shares of stock** in IBM, General Electric, Microsoft, and other corporations. When the market values of those bonds and stocks change, the mark-to-market accounting principle does not raise any issues.

But what about assets for which there is no real day-to-day market? In other words, what about assets that are highly **illiquid?** Many of the assets based on subprime and Alt-A mortgages—all those MBSs, ABSs, and CDOs—were extremely illiquid. Beginning late in 2007, it became clear that some of the underlying mortgages on which those investment securities were based were not going to be paid off in full. But no one knew how many would not be paid off or which ones would go into **default.** And because there was little trading in securities that were based on the mortgages, no one really knew how much they were worth.

Regulators started pressing investment banks and other financial institutions to mark to market. But how was this to be done without any real markets in many of these securities? Enter the computer-modeling wizards again. They put new parameters into their computer valuation models, and presto—they came up with massive downward revaluations of the assets (and thus net worth) of financial institutions. Overnight, some of these financial institutions publicly announced that they had just lost billions of dollars. They actually had not yet lost them, but the computer models, using the mark-to-market accounting principle, generated "paper losses" that staggered the minds of investors throughout the world.

Auditors of financial institutions were worried about overstating the market values of any investments based on subprime mortgage loans. So they continued to drastically reduce the **book value** of anything that resembled a subprime mortgage. Thus the use of the mark-to-market accounting principle quickly became a weapon of mass destruction in the world's financial sector. Within a short period of time, investors lost confidence in some of the largest financial institutions around the world.

THE END OF INVESTMENT BANKING

Many financial institutions went below their required **capital ratios**—the ratio of assets to debt. They needed to raise new capital. They did so by offering new shares of stock for sale. Once the national investment-rating agencies saw those companies in need of new capital, the agencies started reducing these companies' credit ratings, making it more difficult for them to obtain financing and putting more pressure on them to sell assets. These sales in turn reduced the value of their assets, which reduced their ratings. A vicious circle ensued.

Wall Street investment banks—Bear Stearns, Goldman Sachs, Lehman Brothers, Merrill Lynch, and Morgan Stanley—were major players in the mortgage-securities markets. Rising defaults on mortgages, combined with the widespread application of the mark-to-market principle, caused a rapid decline in the values of the securities based on mortgages. Much of this accelerated in 2007 and early 2008 when the investment banks still had positive **cash flows.** But the rapidly declining book value of the assets of investment banks caused other market participants to lose confidence in them. In short order, Bear Stearns found itself no longer a viable entity (and was ultimately purchased by JP Morgan Chase, a **commercial bank**). Not long thereafter, Merrill Lynch sold out to Bank of America. Lehman Brothers went bankrupt. The remaining two large investment banks, Goldman Sachs and Morgan Stanley, became commercial banks. In a matter of weeks, the U.S. investment-banking industry ceased to exist.

In the end, U.S. financial institutions had to **write off** many *hundreds* of billions of dollars, calling them losses. But most of these losses were based solely on computer models rather than on asset transactions. As one analyst pointed out, if the mark-to-market accounting principle had been in effect during the early 1990s when commercial banks found themselves in trouble, every major commercial bank in the United States would have collapsed.

The mark-to-market rule was eased a bit in 2009, but the basic principle remains in place.

BRINGING DOWN AN INSURANCE GIANT

One of the largest insurance companies in the world, American International Group (AIG), also fell victim to overreliance on computer modeling. AIG became a big player in selling a type of insurance against defaults (nonpayment of interest or principal) on all sorts of debts. This insurance is known as **credit-default swaps.** AIG (and many other insurance companies) devised computer models to gauge the risk in its $400 billion portfolio of credit-default swaps.

But these computer models did not take into account abrupt changes in market conditions. In December 2007, the head of AIG, Martin Sullivan, assured AIG's investors that they need not be concerned about exposure to credit-default swaps. Why? Because the company's computer models gave it "a very high level of comfort."

As the master investor Warren Buffett once said, "Beware of geeks bearing formulas." And indeed, AIG's computer formulas turned out to be dead wrong. The federal government had to swoop in to keep AIG afloat. Initially, the government said it was guaranteeing $83 billion of debt at AIG, only later to explain that it had to guarantee more than $200 billion. By 2009, a horde of other insurance companies were asking the federal government for help.

THE WOBBLY STOCK MARKET

Some analysts say that the wildest month in the history of Wall Street ended on October 31, 2008. What no one disputes is that October was the worst month in twenty-one years, as measured by the Standard & Poor's Index of 500 stocks. In contrast, the final week of October 2008 was the best week for the market in thirty-four years. And overall, October 2008 will go down as the most volatile in the eighty-year history of the S&P 500, capping a year that also ranks among the worst in history in terms of both performance and volatility. The most important single factor driving this volatility was this concern: What were trillions of dollars of assets tied to the housing market really worth?

Of course, no one could have reliably predicted what was going to happen to stock prices in 2008. What is certain, though, is that investors reading about hundreds of billions of dollars in losses (even if they were just on paper) could not be expected to have much confidence in the short-term business future in America or elsewhere. And certainly investors were anticipating that declining housing prices were likely to help push the economy into a recession that would likely last for much more than a few months.

The full history of the Panic of '08 is yet to be written. Here is what we do know. There is no doubt that there was a massive downward revision in asset values of all types in 2008, and there was a financial panic of the sort not seen since the 1930s. But the long-run impact of the Panic of '08 on the U.S. and world economies remains uncertain. We can be pretty sure, nonetheless, that a new Great Depression is not around the corner. During the Great Depression of the 1930s, the Federal Reserve allowed the **money supply** in circulation to decrease by one-third. Under Herbert Hoover's leadership, the federal government implemented the Smoot-Hawley Tariff Act, which helped reduce world trade and depressed the economy of the United States. Under President Franklin Roosevelt's leadership, the federal government created legislation and **institutions** that actually raised prices and suppressed private employment.

The federal government has yet to do any of these in response to the Panic of '08—at least so far.

FOR CRITICAL ANALYSIS

1. When might it be important for you, as an individual or household, to use the mark-to-market accounting principle in assessing your own net worth?

2. Do you think that the rating agencies, all of which had bestowed AAA ratings (or the equivalent) on many financial assets that dropped dramatically in value in 2008, should be held liable for investors' losses? Why or why not?

3. The financial meltdown in the United States quickly spread to the rest of the world, particularly to western Europe. It turns out that many large financial institutions throughout the world had invested heavily in mortgage-backed securities, asset-backed securities, and collateralized debt obligations. They, too, had to start writing down the values of these investments, just as financial institutions had done in the United States. What could have enticed so many institutions throughout the world to invest so heavily in securities based on subprime mortgages in the United States?

CHAPTER 9

The Case of the Disappearing Workers

Every month, the Bureau of Labor Statistics (BLS) goes out into the labor market to determine how many unemployed people there are in the United States. With the data it acquires, the BLS calculates the **unemployment rate.** This number is a key indication of how well the economy is doing. The unemployment rate is calculated in a seemingly straightforward way: It is the percentage of the total **labor force** that is (1) over age sixteen but not institutionalized or in school and (2) actively seeking employment but has not found it.

The reelection chances of incumbent presidents often hinge on the estimated rate of unemployment. Historically, when the unemployment rate is rising, the president's chances of reelection have been far worse than when the rate is stable or falling. As the old saying goes, "people vote their pocketbooks" (or in this case, their pay stubs).

For this and a variety of other reasons, understanding how the unemployment rate is measured is important for politicians and ordinary citizens alike. Remarkably, however, there is little consensus about the accuracy of unemployment statistics in the United States. First, consider the period when the United States had its greatest measured rate of unemployment—the Great Depression, which started in 1929 and did not end until the start of World War II a decade later.

25 PERCENT UNEMPLOYMENT—HARD TO IMAGINE

If you look at official government statistics on the unemployment rate during the Great Depression, you will find that in some statistical series, the rate hit 25 percent—meaning that one of every four Americans who were part of the labor force could not find a job during the depth of the depression. That high unemployment rate, of course, makes any **recession** since then seem insignificant in terms of the number of people adversely affected.

Some economists, though, are not so sure that one-fourth of the labor force was actually unemployed during the Great Depression. The reason is simple: At that time, the federal government had instituted numerous programs to "put people back to work." These included the Works Progress Administration (WPA), the Civilian Conservation Corps (CCC), and various lesser programs. Government statisticians decided that everyone working in these federally sponsored "make-work" programs would have been unemployed otherwise. Consequently, they decided to count these millions of Americans as unemployed. Michael Darby, an economist at UCLA, subsequently recalculated unemployment statistics for the depth of the Great Depression. After adjusting for people who were actually working but were counted as unemployed, he found a maximum unemployment rate of 17 percent. This number is still the highest we have had in modern times, but it is certainly not one-fourth of the labor force.

How much sense does Darby's adjustment make? The argument against the official government statistics is straightforward: The federal government taxed individuals and businesses to pay workers at the WPA and CCC. Had the federal government not taxed individuals and businesses to pay these new government employees, the private sector would have had more disposable income, more spending, and higher employment. Whether all of those people would have gotten private-sector jobs is impossible to know, but it is clear that the official numbers greatly overstated the true unemployment rate during the Great Depression.

DISCOURAGED WORKERS: A COVER FOR A HIGHER "TRUE" UNEMPLOYMENT RATE?

Certain individuals, after spending some time in the pool of the unemployed, may become discouraged about their future job prospects. They may leave the labor market to go back to school, to retire, to work full-time at home without pay, or just to take some time off. Whichever path they choose, when interviewers from the Bureau of Labor Statistics ask these individuals whether they are "actively looking for a job," they say no. Individuals such as these are often referred to as **discouraged workers.** They might seek work if labor market conditions were better and potential wages were higher, but they have decided that such is not the case, so they have left the labor market. For years, some critics of the officially measured unemployment rate have argued that during recessions, the rising numbers of discouraged workers cause the government to grossly underestimate the actual rate of unemployment.

To get a feel for the labor market numbers, let's look at the 1990s, perhaps one of the greatest periods of rising employment in U.S. history. During that decade, the number of Americans who were unemployed fell by over 5 million. Moreover, far fewer workers settled for part-time jobs. Many who had been retired came back to work, and many of those about to retire continued to work. There were even large numbers of students who left school to take high-paying jobs in the technology sector.

The onset of the 2001 recession produced a turnaround in all of those statistics. The number of unemployed rose by about 2.5 million individuals. The number of part-time workers who indicated that they would like to work full-time rose by over a million. And the proportion of those out of work for more than half a year increased by over 50 percent.

According to some economists, another 2 million workers dropped out of the labor force—the so-called discouraged-worker problem. For example, University of Chicago economist Robert Topel claims, "The unemployment rate does not mean what it did twenty years ago." He argues that employment opportunities for the least skilled workers no longer exist in today's labor market, so such individuals simply left the labor force, discouraged and forgotten by the statisticians who compile the official numbers.

Are Discouraged Workers a Problem?

Other economists argue differently. They note that the labor market is no different from any other market, so we can examine it using **supply** and **demand** analysis, just as we do with any other good or service. The **labor supply curve** is upward-sloping. That means that as overall wages rise (corrected for inflation, of course), the quantity of labor supplied would be expected to increase. After all, when the inflation-corrected price of just about anything else goes up, we observe that the quantity supplied goes up, too. Therefore, argue these economists, the concept of discouraged workers is basically flawed. They say it makes no more sense to talk of discouraged workers than it would to talk of "discouraged apples" that are no longer offered for sale when the price of apples falls.

Because of the upward-sloping supply curve of labor, when **real wages** rise economywide, we expect retirees and those just about to retire to return to or remain in the labor market. We expect students to quit school early if the wages they can earn are relatively high. The opposite must occur when we go into a recession or the economy stagnates. That is to say, with reduced wage growth (or even declines in economywide real wages) and reduced employment opportunities, we expect more young people to stay in school longer, retirees to stay retired, and those about to retire to actually do so. In other words, we expect the same behavior in response to incentives that we observe in all other markets.

DISABILITY INSURANCE AND LABOR FORCE PARTICIPATION

It is also worth noting that some, perhaps many, of the departures from the labor force by low-skill individuals may actually be prompted by certain government programs. We refer here to a portion of the Social Security program that has expanded dramatically over the past twenty years. It involves **disability payments.** Originally established in 1956 as a program to help individuals under age sixty-five who are truly disabled, Social Security Disability Insurance (SSDI) has become the federal government's second-fastest-growing program (after Medicare). The real value of benefits has steadily risen as the Social Security Administration gradually made it easier for individuals to meet the legal criteria for "disabled" status. SSDI now accounts for over $100 billion in federal spending per year. Under SSDI, even individuals who are not truly disabled can receive payments from the government when they do not work.

In addition, because Social Security also offers Supplemental Security Income (SSI) payments for disabled people who have little or no track record in the labor force, some people are calling disability insurance the centerpiece of a new U.S. welfare state. Just consider that since 1990, the number of people receiving disability payments from the Social Security Administration has more than tripled to over 8 million—perhaps not surprising when you consider that the real value of the monthly benefits a person can collect has risen almost 60 percent in the past thirty-five years. The federal government now spends more on disability payments than on food stamps or unemployment benefits.

What does this mean? Simply that people who might have worked through chronic pain or temporary injuries—particularly those without extensive training and education—have chosen to receive a government disability benefit instead. The average Social Security disability payment is about $1,000 a month, tax-free. For many at the lower echelons of the job ladder, $1,000 a month tax-free seems pretty good. Indeed, those receiving disability payments make up the largest group of the 2 million or so who left the labor force during the 2001–2002 recession. And because people respond to incentives, we can be sure of one thing: Whatever happens to the economy in the future, if the real value of disability payments keeps rising, so will the number of people with disabilities.

For Critical Analysis

1. To what extent do you believe that the existence of unemployment benefits increases the duration of unemployment and consequently the unemployment rate? (*Hint:* Use demand analysis and **opportunity cost.**)

2. Is it possible for the unemployment rate to be "too low"? In other words, can you conceive of a situation in which the economy would be worse off in the long run because there is not enough unemployment?

3. It is believed that much of the increase in the number of people collecting SSDI has resulted from decisions by workers at the Social Security Administration (SSA) to make it easier to qualify for benefits. How are the disability rules set by SSA workers likely to change depending on (a) whether the SSA budget is held constant or expands when the number of SSDI recipients rises; (b) the overall state of the economy, especially the unemployment rate; and (c) the likelihood that individuals with disabilities will be discriminated against in the workplace?

CHAPTER 10

Poverty, Wealth, and Equality

In 1960, the poorest 20 percent of households in the United States received a bit over 4 percent of total income. Today, after half a century of government efforts to relieve poverty, the bottom 20 percent receives a bit less than 4 percent of total income. Almost 40 million Americans lived in poverty in 1960; almost 38 million U.S. citizens *still* live in poverty, despite the expenditure of hundreds of billions of dollars in aid for the poor. In the richest country in the world, poverty seems remarkably resilient.

FIRST, THE FACTS

If we are to understand why, we must begin by getting the facts straight. First, even though the *absolute* number of Americans living in poverty has not diminished over the past half-century, population growth has brought a sizable reduction in the *proportion* of impoverished Americans. As conventionally measured, more than 22 percent of Americans lived in poverty in 1960; by 2009, about 13 percent of the population was below the official poverty line.

Second, traditional methods of measuring poverty may be misleading, because they focus solely on the *cash incomes* of individuals. In effect, government statisticians compute a "minimum adequate" budget for families of various sizes—the "poverty line"—and then determine how many people have cash incomes below this line. Yet major components of the federal government's antipoverty efforts come in the form of **in-kind transfers** (transfers of goods and services, rather than cash) such as Medicare, Medicaid, subsidized housing, food stamps, and school lunches. When the dollar value of these in-kind transfers is included in measures of *total* income, the **standard of living** of persons at lower income levels has improved substantially over the years.

There is disagreement over how much of these in-kind transfers should be included in measures of the total income of recipients.[1] Nevertheless, most observers agree that these transfers, plus the **Earned Income Tax Credit** (which gives special **tax rebates** to low-income individuals), are major sources of income for people at the bottom of the income distribution. Adjusting for these transfers and tax credits, it seems likely that over the past fifty years, the proportion of Americans living below the poverty line has been cut almost in half. Just as important, the standard of living for the poorest 20 percent of the population has doubled since the mid-1960s. In short, the incidence of poverty in this country has declined markedly over the past half-century, and individuals who remain officially classified as "poor" have a far higher real standard of living than the poor of the 1960s.

THE IMPACT OF INCOME MOBILITY

Whatever measure of income we use, it is crucial to remember that most Americans exhibit a great deal of **income mobility,** tending to move around in the income distribution over time. The most important source of income mobility is the "life-cycle" pattern of earnings: New entrants to the workforce tend to have lower incomes at first, but most workers can enjoy rising incomes as they gain experience on the job. Typically, annual earnings reach a maximum at about age fifty-five. Because peak earnings occur well beyond the **median age** of the population (now about age thirty-seven), a "snapshot" of the current distribution of earnings will find most individuals "on the way up" toward a higher position in the income distribution. People who have low earnings now are likely, on average, to have higher earnings in the future.

Another major source of income mobility stems from the operation of Lady Luck. At any point in time, the income of high-income people is likely to be abnormally high (relative to what they can expect on average) due to recent good luck—say, because they just won the lottery or

---

1. There are two reasons for this disagreement. First, a given dollar amount of in-kind transfers is generally less valuable than the same dollar amount of cash income, because cash offers the recipient a greater amount of choice in his or her consumption pattern. Second, medical care is an important in-kind transfer to the poor. Inclusion of all Medicaid expenditures for the poor would imply that the sicker the poor got, the richer they would be. Presumably, a correct measure would include only those medical expenses that the poor would have to incur if they were *not* poor and so had to pay for the medical care (or medical insurance) out of their own pockets.

just received a generous bonus. Conversely, the income of people who currently have low incomes is likely to be abnormally low due to recent bad luck—for example, because they are laid up after an automobile accident or have become temporarily unemployed. Over time, the effects of Lady Luck tend to average out across the population. Accordingly, people with high income today will tend to have lower income in the future, while people with low income today will tend to have higher future income; equivalently, many people living below the poverty line are there temporarily rather than permanently.

The importance of income mobility is strikingly revealed in studies examining the incomes of individuals over time. During the 1970s and 1980s, for example, among the people who were in the top 20 percent (quintile) of income earners at the beginning of the decade, fewer than half were in the top quintile by the end of the decade. Similarly, among the people who were in the bottom quintile at the beginning of the decade, almost half had moved out of that bracket by the end of the decade. Despite news stories that suggest otherwise, income mobility remains robust. From 1996 to 2005 (the decade most recently studied), *more than half* of the people who were in the bottom 20 percent income bracket in 1996 had moved out of that bracket by 2005.

APPEARANCES VERSUS REALITY

Nothwithstanding the data just cited, several forces have either increased income inequality in the United States or have given the appearance of such an increase, so it is best to be clear about these. Consider first that a rising proportion of the population is *far* above the poverty line. In 1969, for example, only about 4 percent of all people in America had incomes seven times greater than the poverty-line level. Today, about 20 percent of Americans have incomes that high (above $150,000 for a family of four). Much of this jump in incomes at the top of the income distribution has come at the very top. Thirty years ago, for example, people in the top 10 percent of earners in America pulled in about 31 percent of total income; today, they garner 37 percent. In even more rarified company, the top 1 percent of earners used to account for 9 percent of total income; today, they take in 16 percent of income. So even though inflation-adjusted incomes are rising across the board, they appear to be rising the fastest at the very top. Economists are seeking to explain this pattern, which first became apparent during the 1990s. Much work remains to be done, but a few answers are emerging.

First, some key demographic changes are occurring in America. The nation is aging, and an older population tends to have more income inequality than a young population because older people have had more time to experience rising or falling fortunes. Americans are also becoming better educated, and this tends to increase income inequality. People with little education have incomes that tend to cluster together, while the incomes of well-educated people spread out: Some choose to convert their **human capital** into much higher incomes, while others convert it into added leisure time. Taken together, these two demographic changes, aging and education, can account for more than 75 percent of the *appearance* of greater income inequality.

Second, a substantial part of the rapid income growth at the top has really been a matter of accounting fiction rather than reality. Until the late 1980s, there were substantial tax advantages for the very wealthy to have a large portion of their incomes counted as corporate income rather than personal income; in effect, a big chunk of income for the wealthy used to be hidden not from the tax authorities but from the policymakers who worry about the distribution of income. Subsequent changes in the tax laws have since encouraged people to report this income as personal rather than corporate income. Their incomes haven't really changed; it just looks to policymakers like they have.

The third factor we need to account for is the difference in consumption bundles of those near the top of the income distribution and those near the bottom. High-income individuals tend to spend a larger proportion of their incomes on labor-intensive services (such as investment advice, personal care, and domestic help). Low-income individuals tend to spend a larger share of their incomes on nondurable goods, such as food, clothing, shoes, and toiletries. As it turns out, over the past twenty-five years, the items consumed by lower-income individuals have fallen markedly in cost relative to the items consumed by the wealthy. Rising **real wages** have pushed up the costs of service-intensive consumption, while growing international trade with China, India, and other developing nations has pushed down the relative costs of items important to low-income individuals. Overall, this difference in **inflation** rates between the people at the top and those at the bottom of the income distribution has effectively wiped out *all* of the seeming change in their relative incomes over this period.

LIFE AT THE BOTTOM

Nevertheless, it is clear that many people at the bottom of the income distribution are struggling, so we need to take a look at what is going on here. One point is clear: Between 1990 and 2007, the United States experienced a huge influx of immigrants. Newcomers typically earn far less than long-term residents. When large numbers of them are added to the mix of people whose incomes are being measured, *average* income can fall, even when the incomes of all individuals are rising. Thus immigration has created downward pressure on *measured* incomes at the bottom of the distribution. But new immigrants have also added to competitive pressures in labor markets for less skilled individuals. On balance, it appears that immigration has probably lowered the wages of high school dropouts in America by 4 to 8 percent. And although this seems small, remember that it is occurring among people whose incomes are already low. Both of these effects are likely to lessen and perhaps even reverse due to the recession of 2007–2009 because deteriorating economic conditions in America caused many recent immigrants to return to their homelands.

Public policy has also taken its toll on the incomes of people at the bottom. The war on drugs, for example, has saddled millions of individuals with criminal records, and the impact has been disproportionately greatest on African Americans, whose incomes were lower to begin with. For example, since 1990, more than 2 million African American males have served time in jail on serious (felony) drug charges. Once they return to the workforce, they find that their felony records exclude them from a great many jobs—and not just jobs at the top. Often convicted felons cannot find positions that pay more than $8 per hour. The result is that the incomes of such individuals are sharply diminished, which means more poverty.

There is one bright spot on the poverty policy front, however. It is the "welfare reform" program undertaken in 1996. Previously, low-income families had been eligible to receive—for an unlimited duration—federal payments called Aid to Families with Dependent Children (AFDC). The program was converted in 1996 into Temporary Assistance to Needy Families (TANF). Limits were placed on the length of time individuals could receive payments, and all recipients were given additional incentives and assistance to enhance their job skills and to enter or reenter the **labor force.** The full impact of this policy change is still being studied, but it now appears that it has modestly raised incomes among those at the bottom of the income distribution.

Although the resilience of poverty in America is discouraging to the poor and to those who study their plight, it is useful to consider these issues in an international context. In other industrialized nations, such as Japan and most countries in Europe, people at the bottom of the income distribution sometimes (but not always) fare better than the poor in America. Although the poor typically receive a somewhat larger *share* of national income than in America, the national income they share is lower.

Hence compared to America, the poorest 10 percent of the population has a higher average income in Japan and Germany but a lower average income in the United Kingdom and Italy.

In developing nations—which is to say, for the vast majority of people around the world—poverty has a completely different meaning than it does in America. In Africa and much of Asia, for example, it is commonplace for people at the bottom of the income distribution to be living on the equivalent of $400 per *year* or less—in contrast to the $10,000 to $15,000 per year they would earn in America. As you saw in Chapter 5, "Poverty, Capitalism, and Growth," this staggering difference in living standards is due to the vast differences in legal and economic **institutions** that are observed around the world. In America, as in many other industrialized nations, these institutions give people the incentives to put their talents to work and also protect the fruits of their labors from expropriation by the government. Thus the best antipoverty program anyone has ever seen is the creation of an institutional environment in which human beings are able to make maximum use of the talents with which they are endowed.

FOR CRITICAL ANALYSIS

1. Why do most modern societies try to reduce poverty? Why don't they do so by simply passing a law that requires that everybody have the same income?

2. How do the "rules of the game" help determine who will be poor and who will not? (*Hint:* How did the Civil Rights Act of 1964, which forbade discrimination on the basis of race, likely affect the incomes of African Americans compared to the incomes of white Americans?) Explain your answer.

3. Which of the following possible in-kind transfers do you think raises the "true" incomes of recipients the most: (a) free golf lessons, (b) free transportation on public buses, or (c) free food? Why?

4. Consider three alternative ways of helping poor people obtain better housing: (a) government-subsidized housing that costs $6,000 per year; (b) a housing **voucher** worth $6,000 per year toward rent on an apartment or a house; or (c) $6,000 per year in cash. Which would you prefer if you were poor? On what grounds might you make your decision?

CHAPTER 11

Will It Be Inflation or Deflation?

During the summer of 2008, when gas prices were skyrocketing, the Department of Labor issued a frightening statistic: The **consumer price index (CPI)** had risen more than 5 percent over the prior twelve months, the biggest jump in nearly twenty years. A few months later, the average price of gasoline paid in the United States had dropped from over $4 per gallon to well under $2 per gallon. And as the price of gas was plummeting, **inflation** among primary commodities (such as lumber, metals, and grain) was collapsing as well. As a result, in the late summer and early fall, the overall inflation rate shrank to almost nothing; in fact, during several months in late 2008 and early 2009, overall consumer prices actually *fell*—there was **deflation.** This rapid turn of events quickly switched the Web site and news channel chatter about the problems of inflation into chatter about the prospects for sustained deflation. Before we try to sort out whether inflation or deflation is in your future, let's first make sure we know to what we are referring.

A FORMAL DEFINITION OF INFLATION AND DEFLATION

Inflation is defined as a rise in the average of all prices, appropriately weighted for their importance in the typical consumer's budget. Inflation is not a change in one price. If the CPI rises by 3 percent over a twelve-month period, what we know is that the appropriately weighted average of prices of goods and services in the United States went up by 3 percent relative to a year before. (Sometimes you will see references to **core inflation.** This is a measure of the overall change in prices *excluding energy and food.*)

If the rate of change in the **price level** is negative rather than positive, we have deflation—on average, prices are falling rather than rising. As our brief introduction suggests, people worry a lot about inflation, but they also worry about deflation. So we must ask, are these concerns misplaced?

THE DOWNSIDE OF DEFLATION

Deflation can be troublesome for the economy. One reason is that most of the debts in a modern society like ours are expressed in terms of dollars. When there is deflation, the **real purchasing power** of those dollars goes up. For creditors, this is good news, because it means that people now owe them more, measured in terms of the goods and services those dollars will buy (so-called *real* terms). But for debtors, this is bad news, for exactly the same reason. Deflation raises the real burden of the debts they owe. Debtors have to pay back the sums owed with dollars that have a higher purchasing power than the dollars that were lent. In effect, during times of deflation, the inflation-corrected rate of interest (the **real interest rate**) goes up, imposing an added burden on debtors. Although it is possible that deflation's positive effects on creditors and negative effects on debtors could exactly cancel out, often it doesn't happen this way. The result can be significant economic dislocations.

There is also another problem with deflation. It never proceeds evenly and smoothly. During the Great Depression, when prices fell an *average* of about 8 percent per year for four straight years, this deflation did not proceed uniformly over time; some months and years were worse than others. Moreover, the deflation did not proceed uniformly across all goods; house prices, for example, fell much more than clothing prices. Because of the erratic and unpredictable progression of deflation, individuals and businesses had to focus much of their attention on trying to predict the magnitude and timing of changes in the prices of goods and services. Had there been no deflation, they could have been producing new goods and services instead. The result was that the U.S. economy had fewer goods and services available for **consumption.**

THE COSTS OF INFLATION

Inflation acts as a tax on people's holdings of money—that is, their holdings of **currency** and **checkable deposits.** All of us hold some currency and checkable deposits because of the convenience they provide. As a result, each of us loses **wealth** whenever there is inflation, because the purchasing power of our money balances decreases at the rate of inflation.

Assume that you have $20 stashed in your wallet as an emergency cash reserve; that is, you have no immediate expectation of spending it. If at the end of one year there has been a 10 percent rise in the price level, the purchasing power of that $20 note will only be $18, measured in terms of taxi rides or sandwiches. You will have lost value equal to 10 percent times the amount of currency you kept in your wallet.

In essence, then, the purchasing power, or real value, of the money we hold depreciates when there is inflation. The only way we can avoid this type of **inflation tax** on the money we hold is to reduce our holdings of money. But doing this is not an easy matter. It is beneficial—productive—to have money on hand to pay for the things that we want when we want them rather than trying to purchase everything at the beginning of a pay period so as to minimize the dollars in our checkable accounts or in our wallets.

Thus one cost to society of inflation is that it increases the cost of holding money. For society as a whole, we therefore use *too little* money during periods of inflation. This effect is greatest for currency, because its real value falls one-for-one with each rise in the price level. The tax is much less for checkable deposits, because many of these accounts pay some interest, and that **nominal interest rate** rises when the expected inflation rate rises.

We should also add that periods of inflation generate exactly the sort of prediction problems that arise when there is deflation. Inflation never proceeds evenly across time or across goods. As a result, during periods of inflation, consumers and businesses must spend some of their time trying to predict exactly how the inflation is likely to proceed. And this in turn means they are spending less time producing output that is available for consumption.

INFLATION, DEFLATION, AND THE MONEY SUPPLY

Throughout the history of the world, there has been a fairly consistent long-run relationship between the change in the price level over time and the change in the **money supply**—money in circulation. This relationship does not move in lockstep fashion in the short run. But it does hold, on average, over longer periods of time, and it is *sustained* inflation or deflation that is a cause for the greatest concern.

There are several ways to define a country's money supply; for our purposes, let's treat it as currency plus all of the funds in accounts that can be used for transactions, such as those accessible with debit cards. As already noted, a predictable long-term relationship has been observed between changes in the money supply and changes in the general price level: sustained, rapid monetary growth yields inflation, and sustained shrinkage in the money supply causes deflation. **Expansive monetary policy** on the part of the **Federal Reserve** caused the money supply to increase quite rapidly after the short **recession** in 2001–2002, for example. The expansion in the money supply continued through the decade. Not surprisingly, inflation crept upward, from 1.6 percent in 2001 to over 4 percent in 2007. And as inflation rose, so did concerns over how bad it would get.

DEFLATION DISCUSSIONS FRONT AND CENTER

The talk of inflation came to a screeching halt at the end of the summer of 2008. Partly it was those plummeting gas and commodity prices that took the steam out of the inflation talk. But the financial panic of 2008 also changed sentiments about the likely course of the price level in 2009 and beyond.

Indeed, all of Washington, D.C., and the financial world suddenly started worrying about deflation. According to Professor Frederic Mishkin of Columbia University, "If inflation expectations were to decline sharply, that would greatly increase the risk of deflation." Further, according to American Enterprise Institute researcher Desmond Lachman, "A deep and prolonged recession could raise the specter of deflation of the sort that plagued the Japanese economy." Lachman was referring to the 1990s, when Japan experienced a flat or declining price level (some economists refer to this as Japan's "lost decade").

Will this talk of deflation turn out to be reality as you are reading these words? We are skeptical. Among other things, the Fed reacted to the Panic of '08 with much easier credit policies, injecting more money into the economy. Initially, banks were not very amenable to lending out these new funds, so there were few signs of inflationary pressure early in 2009. But unless the Fed manages to move these funds out of the system as the economy recovers from the recession, inflationary trouble lies ahead.

So here is our prediction, notwithstanding the dire predictions of falling prices. Deflation may be in your future, but if so, only for a relatively short time. Inflation, at least in the long run, is more likely. Eventually, all the increases in the money supply that were made possible by the Fed's credit expansion in 2008 will be realized in 2010 and beyond. Once the economy starts moving again, particularly the financial sector, banks will start lending their **excess reserves.** The money supply will be growing again, and the price level will be rising. So in the short run, you may see a bit of both rising and falling prices, but over the long haul, we would bet that you have mostly inflation to look forward to.

FOR CRITICAL ANALYSIS

1. When the price of a barrel of petroleum increased greatly in 2008, every news article about rising oil prices had a negative slant. When the price of petroleum dropped by more than half later in the year, the press said little, and much of what the press said was negative. Those negative comments focused on fears that there would not be enough new exploration for oil in the future. Is it really possible for a rise in the price of a good to be "bad" and also for a drop in the price of that same good to be "bad"?

2. If the inflation rate is fully anticipated, what are the ways in which consumers and businesses can protect against the resulting loss of purchasing power?

3. Who are the people who are most affected by unanticipated inflation? Why?

CHAPTER 12

Is It Real, or Is It Nominal?

Every few years, some important commodity, such as gasoline, electricity, or food, experiences a spike in prices. Reporters examine such price spikes and plaster newspapers, magazines, and Web sites with the appropriate headlines—sometimes relentlessly, day after day. TV commentators interview frustrated and worried Americans who spout the expected negative reactions to the higher prices of essential items in their budgets. The world, it would seem, is coming to an end.

Was Gas Really Expensive?

Let's just take one often-in-the-press example, gasoline prices. The authors of the book you are reading are old enough to remember the TV interviews that ensued when the price of gas first hit the unprecedented level of $1 per gallon, back in 1980. The same types of interviews occurred when the price of a gallon of gas broke the $2 barrier, early in 2005, and lodged above $3 in 2007. Not surprisingly, virtually the same types of interviews occurred when the price of a gallon of gas rose above $4 in the summer of 2008. At each point in time, everyone interviewed had the same response, even though years had passed between the different price spikes: "I guess I'll just have to stop driving." "I'm going to get a bike." "I'm selling my big car and getting a small one." And of course, each time there was an accompanying story about how record numbers of people were (or soon would be) flocking to their neighborhood motor scooter dealerships.

If we wish to sensibly analyze the effects of higher prices on the quantity demanded and the quantity supplied of any good or service in this world, we can rely neither on what journalists report nor on what

Americans say when they are interviewed. After all, what is important is not what people say but what they do. As economists, we best understand consumers by their **revealed preferences**. Similarly, businesspeople are best understood by their actions, not their words. What people do is reflected in how much they actually buy of any good or service after its price changes, not by their complaints to a TV reporter or what they post on their blog or on Facebook or MySpace.

RELATIVE PRICES, NOMINAL PRICES, AND INFLATION

For both microeconomic and macroeconomic analysis, the relevant price is the price *relative to* all other prices, because people's decisions are based on **relative prices,** not **nominal prices.** The latter simply tell us the number of pieces of paper (dollar bills) you must hand over for a good. Nominal prices tell us nothing about the real sacrifice (measured in terms of goods or labor services) that one must make to obtain those goods. Relative prices reflect the real sacrifice involved in acquiring a good because they tell us the price of a good or service relative to the price of another good or service or to the average of all other prices. Relative prices tell us how much of other goods we must sacrifice.

Said another way, we have to separate out the rise in the general price level, called **inflation,** and the rise in the nominal price of a particular good or service. If *all* nominal prices went up exactly 3 percent, there would be no change in relative prices. This inflation of 3 percent per year would not change the real sacrifice entailed in acquiring any particular good. In the real world, even during periods of inflation, some prices go up faster than others and some prices even go down—witness the price of computing power, DVD players, and MP3 players. Nevertheless, if we want to predict people's behavior, we must know what has happened to the *relative* price of a good, and to determine this, we must adjust for inflation.

GAS PRICES REVISITED

Now let's get back to our example of gasoline prices. Your grandparents might be able to talk about buying gas for 30 cents a gallon (its average nominal price most of the time between 1956 and 1964). Today, what you pay in dollars per gallon is many times that level. People still drive nonetheless—indeed, the use of gasoline for cars and trucks in the United States is roughly triple what it was when the nominal price of gas was only 30 cents. Something must have happened. The most important "something" is a general rise in all prices, including gasoline prices.

In the summer of 2008, the price of gasoline spiked over $4 per gallon. Presidential candidate Barack Obama argued that the government should intervene on gas prices to "give families some relief." Two-thirds of American voters at that time said they thought that the price of gas was "an extremely important political issue." (Of course, when gas prices started tumbling in the fall of 2008, there were not many front-page articles or TV interviews with happy consumers. And the politicians simply became silent on this subject.) Consider, though, that at its nominal price at the beginning of 2009, the *relative* price of gas was back down to about what it had been in 1960—after correcting for overall inflation. For many people, this is a shocking revelation. But correcting for inflation is absolutely essential if you want to sensibly analyze the price of anything over time. Often we talk about the **real price** of a good or service. This refers specifically to subtracting the rate of inflation from the change in a nominal price over time. Not surprisingly, we also do the same exercise when we want to go from **nominal income** to **real income** over time.

THE IMPORTANCE OF HIGHER DISPOSABLE INCOME

Another fact is particularly relevant when thinking about the real burden of gasoline. People are becoming more productive over time because they are getting better educated and because ongoing technological change enables us to produce more with a given input of our time. As a result of this higher **productivity,** U.S. consumers' **disposable incomes** generally rise from one year to the next—and certainly rise on average over longer periods of time. As Americans become richer on average, they are financially able to handle even higher relative prices of those items they wish to purchase, gasoline included.

To help us understand this point better, researchers Indur Goklany and Jerry Taylor came up with an "affordability index." They compared family income to the price of gas from 1949 to 2008. They arbitrarily set 1960 at an affordability index of 1; relative to this, a higher affordability index number means that something is more affordable. Even when gas was $4.15 per gallon, the affordability gas index was 1.35. In other words, the ratio of the average person's disposable income to the price of gasoline was higher by about 35 percent in 2008 than it was in 1960—gasoline was *more* affordable than it had been back in 1960, when your grandparents were filling up their tanks at 30 cents a gallon. That's hard to believe for some of us but true nonetheless. And once gas prices started going down at the end of 2008, the gas affordability index rose even more, passing 2, meaning that gasoline was more than twice as affordable at the beginning of 2009 as it had been in 1960.

PRODUCT QUALITY CHANGES

The quality of gasoline typically does not change much over time. But the quality of many other products often changes significantly over time, usually for the better. Often we forget about this crucial aspect when we start comparing prices of a good or service over time. If you ask senior citizens today how much they paid for their first car, you might get prices in the range of $2,000 to $5,000. The average new car today costs around $24,000 (in nominal dollars). By now, of course, you know that if you want to compare these numbers, you have to first account for the inflation that has occurred over whatever time period you are examining. In this case, adjusting for inflation still means that the relative price of a car appears to be about 30 percent higher than it was, say, fifty years ago.

Does that necessarily mean that a car is really 30 percent more expensive than it was in 1960? Probably not. We must take into account improved quality features of cars today compared to those of fifty years ago. Today (unlike fifty years ago), the average car has the following:

- Antilock computer-controlled power brakes
- Power steering
- Digital radio with CD or MP3 player
- Air conditioning
- Steel-belted radial tires
- Cruise control
- Power windows and locks
- Air bags
- Forty percent better fuel economy

The list of improved and new features is actually much longer. Today, the average car is safer, breaks down less often, needs fewer tune-ups, has a host of amenities that were not even dreamed of fifty years ago—and almost certainly lasts for at least twice as many miles. If you correct not only for inflation but also for these quality increases, the relative price of cars today has almost certainly *fallen* appreciably in the past fifty years, in spite of the "sticker shock" that you may experience when you go shopping for a new car. That is, appearances to the contrary, the inflation-corrected **constant-quality price** of automobiles is actually lower today than it was five decades ago.

Declining Nominal Prices

The necessity of adjusting for inflation and quality changes continues to apply even when we are examining goods whose nominal prices have declined over time. A good example is computing power. The nominal price of the average personal computer has gone down in spite of general inflation over the past several decades. These days, a Windows-based desktop computer has an average price of about $550; for a laptop, the average price is a bit over $700. A decade ago, the average machines in each category would have had nominal prices of twice as much. You might be tempted to conclude, then, that the price of personal computing has fallen by 50 percent. You'd be wrong: The price has actually fallen by more than 50 percent.

Why? There are two reasons. First, over the past ten years, the average dollar prices of all goods increased by 30 percent; that is how much overall inflation there has been. That means that the *relative* price of the average computer has fallen by two-thirds, which, of course, is greater than 50 percent. But even here we are missing something extremely important: The quality of what you are buying—computing power—has skyrocketed. The processor speed of the average computer today is at least ten times greater than it was ten years ago and is increasing exponentially. Moreover, hard drives are bigger, monitors are flat-screen LCDs instead of bulky old cathode ray tubes, laptops are lighter, RAM is larger—the list of improvements goes on and on. And despite people's frustrations with both the hardware and software of the personal computer today, longtime users can tell you that both are vastly more reliable than they were a decade ago. Thus if you only look at the inflation-corrected decrease in computer prices, you will be underestimating the *true* decrease in the relative price of computers.

The moral of our story is simple. At some point in your education, you learned that "what goes up must come down." Now you know that when it comes to prices, it is often the case that "what goes up has actually gone done." It is a lesson worth keeping in mind if you really want to understand the behavior of consumers and businesses alike.

For Critical Analysis

1. Create a list of goods (or services) whose quality has improved over time in such a way that the current prices of these commodities do not accurately reflect their real prices, even after adjusting for inflation. Now see if you can come up with a list of items whose quality has systematically *decreased* over time. Can you suggest why it is easier to find examples of the former than the latter?

2. The demand for small-engine motor scooters jumped when the price of gasoline started moving up in the summer of 2008. Make a prediction about the demand for this form of transportation in, say, two years from today. Explain your answer.

3. Explain why you will make more accurate predictions if you focus on the changing incentives people face rather than listening to what they say they are going to do.

PART THREE
Fiscal Policy

CHAPTER 13

The Growth of Big Government

In 1996, the forty-second president of the United States, William Jefferson Clinton, declared, "The era of big government is over." Whatever else President Clinton may have been, he was not a prophet. Shortly after he made this declaration, **discretionary spending** by the federal government accelerated at a torrid pace.

DISCRETIONARY VERSUS NONDISCRETIONARY GOVERNMENT SPENDING

Spending by the federal government and some state governments can be divided into two types: discretionary and nondiscretionary. Discretionary spending is anything that Congress decides to spend for which it has to appropriate monies in its **appropriation bills** each **fiscal year.** A good example of discretionary spending is the $30 billion spent to help New York City and various private firms that suffered greatly from the terrorist attacks on September 11, 2001. Nondiscretionary spending is usually driven by **entitlement programs.** These are *formula-driven* expenditures. The best examples are Social Security and Medicare, which provide specific formulas, or rules, that automatically decide who is eligible and the amount for which they are eligible. Once the law is passed that dictates the amount to which individuals are entitled, Congress no longer controls the amount of funds spent on these programs. The only way such nondiscretionary spending can be slowed down or speeded up is if Congress changes the formulas that dictate who gets what and how much they get.

At the time Bill Clinton made his pronouncement, discretionary spending had indeed fallen slightly from 1994 through part of 1995. It was hovering around $550 billion per year. But by 2008, such spending was in the neighborhood of *double* that amount. And that was *before* the $800 billion economic bailout plan or the new infrastructure and other "stimulus" spending that started in 2009. So much for the end of big government!

IS 9/11 TO BLAME?

One can reasonably (but misleadingly) argue that since September 11, 2001, the federal government and state and local governments have had to spend more on antiterrorism measures. Though this statement is true in one sense, the overall government-spending picture, particularly at the federal level, is quite different. For six years before the terrorist attacks, total federal discretionary spending had already been rising rapidly. This spending was eventually supplemented by funds that were voted for spending on homeland security and national defense. But these supplements were a small blip on the radar screen of total increases in federal discretionary spending. Roughly $30 billion was spent on homeland security and national defense programs in the months following 9/11. But in fiscal year 2002, Congress voted an additional $90 billion of new discretionary spending, which included funds for medical research and highway construction. Fiscal years 2003 through 2007 all witnessed further additions to federal discretionary spending.

What has been true and will continue to be true into the foreseeable future is that numerous expenditures that have absolutely nothing to do with countering terrorism will be approved in the name of the fight against terrorism. Consider the latest set of "gifts" to the farming sector, one of the most brazen examples of how old-fashioned special interest **subsidies** can be hidden under the cover of the war on terrorism. Since 1978, farmers have received subsidies of $400 billion from the federal government. In recognition of the huge amount of spending going to this tiny **interest group,** Congress in 1996 passed the Freedom to Farm bill, which was intended to phase out subsidies to farmers gradually. Yet not only have the subsidies *increased* since then, but members of Congress from farm states have also used the war on terrorism as a pretext to ask for even more. How have they done this? By including the word *security* in the title of the farm bill to link the "insecurity" that farmers are currently feeling about their future incomes to the insecurity that Americans in general are feeling in the wake of the terrorist attacks.

The latest farm legislation, passed in 2008, is expected to cost U.S. taxpayers and consumers at least $30 billion per year. The Farm Security and Rural Investment Act, its full title, was the largest agricultural subsidy in the history of the United States—foisted on the public in the name of increased "security," of course.

Some observers believe that all manner of spending that is packaged under the banner of homeland security will become a permanent addition to our federal spending apparatus. The federal government will, as a consequence, keep getting larger, not smaller.

THE DEPARTMENT OF HOMELAND SECURITY

When President George W. Bush proposed creation of the Department of Homeland Security (DHS), he argued that it would not make government larger. Almost everyone now thinks that President Bush will turn out to be no better as a prognosticator than his predecessor. In principle, the DHS has simply combined twenty-two agencies and 170,000 workers to create a more efficient way to protect Americans at home. Realize, though, that this department is the most massive new bureaucracy since the Department of Defense (DOD) was created in 1947. The likelihood of the DHS remaining even close to its original size is small, if not zero.

First, many DHS activities, like DOD activities, are secret. This reduces the chances that spending on them will be carefully scrutinized. Second, DHS and DOD activities are supposed to protect us from people who would do us harm. If a member of Congress stops a project on budget grounds and an unfortunate security breach later occurs as a result, that could be the end of a political career. Finally, DHS activities, like DOD activities, are complex and far-reaching. It is easy to claim—and difficult to refute—that a loss of spending on one project will have spillover effects that will irreparably damage many other projects.

The result with the DOD is a budget that seems largely immune to shrinkage. Furthermore, plenty of private-sector firms have an incentive to keep that budget big because they are doing business with the department. Hence they lobby for additional funding so that they, too, can get some of those extra federal dollars. It is likely that these same incentives will work their magic with the DHS budget. Indeed, within a few months after the DHS asked private corporations to propose new technologies to fight terrorism, some fifteen hundred companies had pitched their ideas. Consider one proposal from an enterprising company: Fit every commercial airline seat with metal straps. Why? To snare potential hijackers. Yet another proposal: Teach transcendental meditation to our enemies. Why? Obviously, to calm them down. The list, one imagines, is still growing.

THE IMPACT OF SOCIAL SECURITY AND MEDICARE SPENDING ON THE FEDERAL BUDGET

So far, we have discussed mainly federal discretionary spending. On the horizon, however, looms a serious and growing problem with two of the most important entitlement programs, Social Security and Medicare. At the beginning of the twenty-first century, actual outlays for Social Security and Medicare were about 6.5 percent of the nation's annual national income, or, as it is commonly called, **gross domestic product (GDP).** That proportion has now risen to 7 percent; by 2025 it will grow to 10 percent and by 2040 to over 12 percent. This increase in spending on these two entitlement programs is due not only to the increased number of retirees from the baby boom generation (born between 1946 and 1964) but also to the aging of the population as a whole, which is projected to continue for the next half-century at least.

The implied burden of this aging and the growing programs is enormous. At the beginning of the twenty-first century, there were 4.3 workers for every person aged sixty-five or over. By 2020, there will be 2.6 workers; by 2050, there will be 2.4; and by 2075, only 2.2. In other words, a working couple will have to provide almost all of the Social Security and Medicare support for each retired person—in addition to supporting themselves and their children. Put somewhat differently, if you think a big piece of your paycheck is going for taxes now, just wait—a much larger piece will be departing in the future.

BAILOUT AT ANY COST

In 2008, federal spending took on an entirely new dimension when, in response to the Panic of '08 (see Chapter 8), Congress passed a $700 billion bailout package for the financial industry. This was followed in 2009 by an additional $800 billion federal stimulus package that was designed, it was said, to pull us out of the recession of 2007–2009. And behind the scenes, the Federal Reserve was busy giving financial institutions more than $1 trillion in government securities in exchange for commercial paper and other risky private-sector debts that could turn out to be largely worthless. Indeed, within a matter of months, Congress and the Fed had committed American taxpayers to $2 *trillion* in potential spending obligations.

Just how much the taxpayer—which is to say, you—will end up paying depends on how many companies default on the various bailout programs. At this point, the exact total is a matter of speculation. It is pretty clear, however, that the sum will be in the many tens of billions of dollars, possibly *hundreds* of billions of dollars. And since 40 percent of all Americans pay *no* federal income taxes, this means that the rest of us will pay plenty. If the **default** rate ends up being as low as 15 percent, a family of four will be hit with an extra tax bill of about $8,000—in addition to its obligation for the rest of the growing government.

THE TRUE SIZE OF GOVERNMENT

Government at any level does not exist independently of the people who live, work, spend, and pay taxes in our society. As an economy, we face a **budget constraint.** Whatever is spent by government—federal, state, and local—cannot be spent by individuals. Fundamentally, when we talk about the "size" of government, we are talking about the proportion, or percentage, of GDP that government commands. Logic dictates that whatever government commands in terms of spending decisions, private individuals do not command. From this perspective (and this is simple arithmetic), federal, state, and local governments command over 40 percent of GDP. In addition, some observers have argued that the various levels of government also compel businesses and individuals to spend an additional 10 percent of total income to comply with government regulations and **mandates.** If we follow this line of reasoning, the implication is that directly or indirectly, government in the United States controls the allocation of over one-half of all **resources**—which leaves less than half for you.

FOR CRITICAL ANALYSIS

1. The Tax Foundation estimated that the direct tax burden of government actually dropped significantly between 2000 and 2004, due chiefly to federal tax cuts in 2003. Based on what you have read in this chapter, do you believe that this decline has continued since 2004 or will continue in the future? Why or why not?

2. Around the world, the percentage of total GDP controlled by the government has a tendency to grow. Why do you think this is so?

3. Although federal taxes were cut twice between 2001 and 2005, federal spending rose over that span, so the amount of debt owed by the federal government increased. What does this higher level of debt imply about the likely tax burden of the federal government in the future?

CHAPTER 14

Debts and Deficits: What's a Trillion More or Less?

How many times have you heard the advice to "stay out of debt"? Certainly, that advice has rarely been followed by your lawmakers in Washington, D.C. Over the past half-century, the federal government has spent within its means during only five years. In the other years, it ran a **federal budget deficit**—that is, it spent more than it received in tax receipts. Now, of course, if you or your family spent more than you earned year-in and year-out, you would eventually go bankrupt. Obviously, this has not happened to the federal government.

DIFFERENT WAYS TO LOOK AT THE FEDERAL BUDGET DEFICIT

The official federal budget deficit can be found in numerous publications, including *The Economic Report of the President*. If you examine the data on the federal deficit for the past twenty years, you see that after shrinking in the 1990s, it has been growing since. To get a handle on the true size of the deficit, though, as you learned in Chapter 12, we must at least take into account changes in the **price level.** When we thus correct for **inflation,** the *real* federal budget deficit from 1989 to 2009 grew by 60 percent less than the nominal value that each year's deficit showed, because the overall price level rose 60 percent.

Over that same time period, something else very important happened. The size of the U.S. economy grew quite handsomely. Consequently, the more revealing statistic concerning the federal budget deficit is how that deficit has changed as a percentage of total economic activity, or **gross domestic product (GDP).** In 1989, the deficit as a share of GDP was 2.8 percent. At the beginning of 2009, it was 2.9 percent. Those two numbers are obviously almost identical—although by the time you read this, the federal deficit will have grown to a *much* larger share of GDP.

THE CRASH OF 2008–2009

Whereas the estimated federal budget deficit was about $450 billion in 2008, by the time you read this, it will have risen to $1 trillion or more. That will represent the largest single one-year increase in the real (inflation-adjusted) deficit in the history of the United States—and the largest jump in the deficit as a share of GDP since World War II. As we write this chapter, we cannot even tell you exactly how big the latest surge in the deficit is because no one yet can predict it.

In response to the financial meltdown of 2008–2009, the federal government legislated so many financial bailouts that the actual amount for which the U.S. taxpayer is on the hook is currently unknowable. Eventually, we will know, of course. To return to our back-of-the-envelope calculations, consider this: Ignoring for the moment the federal takeover of the two enormous government-sponsored mortgage companies, Freddie Mac and Fannie Mae, the 2008 $700 billion bank bailout bill will certainly add another $400 or $500 billion to the 2009 deficit. (The addition to the deficit is less than the official size of the bailout because the government will recoup *something* from the companies we are bailing out.) Add to this President Obama's $800 billion economic "stimulus" package, passed early in 2009, and now you are talking in the trillions, more or less, of course. Thus, realistically speaking, by 2010, the federal budget deficit will be more than *double* what it was in 2008, expressed as a percentage of GDP.

DEFICITS AND DEBT

If you decide to go on an expensive Caribbean vacation, you may not have enough funds currently available to do so. You could borrow at least part of the funds from a consumer finance company or from your bank. This additional borrowing adds to your outstanding debt. The same logic applies to the federal government. Each year that there is a deficit, the **public debt** grows by that amount, because the debt is just the sum of current and past deficits. In the popular press, you often read that the public debt now exceeds $12 trillion. That quoted number is usually meaningless. It refers to the **gross public debt,** which at the beginning of 2009 was $12.7 trillion.

The problem with the gross public debt statistic is that it includes **interagency borrowings.** If one part of the federal government loans funds to another part of the federal government, that loan really has no impact on anybody. Therefore, what we really want to know is the size and growth in the **net public debt.** The net public debt is the gross public debt minus all federal interagency borrowings. At the beginning of 2009, this debt was $8.4 trillion—quite a bit less than the gross public debt.

Are you shocked, even by this smaller number? You might be, but you are still not looking at the most appropriate statistic. As with the federal deficit, we either have to look at the inflation-corrected change in the net public debt over time or at the net public debt as a percentage of GDP. In 1989, the net public debt represented about 40 percent of GDP. At the beginning of 2009, it represented about 50 percent of GDP. What will it be at the beginning of 2010? Well, it is a good bet that it will be substantially more than 50 percent of GDP, but probably not yet at the astronomical 108.6 percent it reached in 1946, just after the end of World War II.

Another way of examining the importance of the net public debt is to first correct for inflation and then correct for the number of Americans. The result is the **per capita real net public debt.** Measured in 2008 dollars, in 1989, this number was $15,500. Early in 2009, it hit $28,000; this is a hefty increase, particularly when you consider that most of the increase occured after 2007.

Unfunded Taxpayer Liabilities

For at least a decade, some politicians and many economists examined with a critical eye the activities of Freddie Mac and Fannie Mae. They pointed out that even though these entities were owned by private shareholders, there was an implicit government guarantee of their obligations. In other words, if they got into trouble, the federal government would come to the rescue. That is why they have always been referred to as **government-sponsored enterprises (GSEs).**

As early as the 1990s, some economists calculated that there was several hundred billion dollars' worth of implicit taxpayer **liabilities** associated with the government's implicit guarantee of these fast-growing mortgage-market institutions. These researchers thought that the implicit future taxpayer liabilities should be added to the net public debt numbers.

As you know by now, the tragic story of the implicit guarantees of their obligations came to be true. The federal government had to take over both companies in the fall of 2008. We're all on the hook, but not for a measly few hundred billion dollars. Rather, it looks as if U.S. taxpayers are committed for these two large organizations to the tune of close to a trillion dollars (that's $1,000,000,000,000). We will not know for several years what the exact number is. What we do know, though, is that the published U.S. government net public debt statistics underestimate the *true* net public debt because of these now obvious and undeniable liabilities.

There is more to this story of **unfunded taxpayer liabilities.** If you look at projected expenditures on Social Security, Medicare, and the federal portion of Medicaid (health care for the poor, partly financed by the state governments), you come up with a number so large you cannot even comprehend it. That number, which is in the tens of trillions of dollars, some 300 or 400 percent of current GDP, represents the unfunded portion of future estimated federal expenditures on the three programs just mentioned.

Because these unfunded federal spending program expenditures are so large, you can be certain of one thing—something will have to give. The long-run problem amounts to an enormous increase in the net public debt—one that is staggering in size, even compared to the massive obligations incurred during the Great Depression and World War II. Eventually, members of Congress, the president, and the public (that would be you) will have to face the music. Only two options are available: Either spending on these programs will have to be cut dramatically, or you will have to sacrifice an unprecedented share of your hard-earned income to pay for the rising retirement and medical expenditures of seniors.

WHO REALLY PAYS FOR CURRENT FEDERAL GOVERNMENT EXPENDITURES?

Some economists believe that discussion of the federal budget deficit is beside the point—a red herring, as it were. Consider a typical year. Total economic activity as measured by GDP is perhaps $16 trillion as you read this. At the local, state, and federal levels of government, numerous expenditures are made. Let's suppose those expenditures equal 40 percent of GDP. Now ask yourself this question: For a typical resident, does the method of paying for government expenditures matter? For example, assume that all of these expenditures are paid for by tax revenues; there are no deficits. You know *explicitly* that as the average U.S. resident, you have given up 40 percent of your annual income to pay for government at all levels.

Consider another scenario. Suppose taxes pay for only a portion of that 40-plus percent of GDP spent by government. Deficit financing pays for the rest. As a typical U.S. resident, you still do not have control over the part of GDP the government spent during the year. Even if only a portion of the 40-plus percent controlled by government is financed via current taxes, you are still on the hook for the rest of it—plus interest, of course. Moreover, however the spending is financed this year, it is still government employees, not you, who get to decide how 40-plus percent of your income is used.

Consider an earlier example when government spending also skyrocketed. During World War II, Americans fought in two simultaneous wars, in the Pacific and in Europe. Not surprisingly, government spending increased dramatically. Many history books talk about how Americans continued paying for World War II for years thereafter because the net public debt rose so much due to high wartime federal borrowing.

But can that really be true? No, it cannot. The people in this country who lived during World War II effectively paid for World War II each year when government expenditures took place. As a percentage of GDP, they ended up with less for themselves. Indeed, the inflation-corrected per capita rate of consumption expenditures dropped during World War II and did not start rising until several years after the end of that war.

In a sentence, the real burden of government is the **resources** it uses, and that burden occurs at the point in time when the resources are used, deficits and debts notwithstanding.

FOR CRITICAL ANALYSIS

1. If you cannot continue to spend more than you earn, why can the federal government?

2. Some economists estimate that if you add the unfunded tax liabilities of just Social Security and Medicare, they add up to about $80 trillion. Do you think that in the long run, this $80 trillion estimate can continue to hold true? Why or why not? (*Hint:* Who pays for unfunded tax liabilities?)

3. Why will the U.S. government never go bankrupt?

CHAPTER 15

Higher Taxes Are in Your Future

"These road improvements of $241,000,000 were paid for:

86 percent from the Federal Highway Trust Fund
12 percent from state funds
2 percent from local funds."

Most of you have seen at least one sign similar to this while driving somewhere in the United States. If you have ever driven anywhere in Europe, you see comparable signs, but they usually have a longer list of "contributors." The parallel, though, is that the "contributors" are government agencies, not *you*. Now, it would be nice to think that funds for highway improvement projects come from the moon or Mars or even from the bank account of some foreign oil mogul. But they do not.

THOSE PESKY BUDGET CONSTRAINTS

Government does not exist independently of those who live, work, spend, and pay taxes in our society. As an economy, we face a **budget constraint.** Whatever is spent by government—federal, state, or local—is not and cannot be spent by individuals in the nation. Whatever government commands in terms of spending decisions, private individuals do not command. All of those dollars available for spending on final goods and services in the United States can be controlled either by you, the private citizen, or by government. Otherwise stated, what the government spends, you don't spend. It is as simple as that, despite the periodic efforts of government (especially at the national level) to conceal the truth of this budget constraint.

FEDERAL SPENDING PROGRAMS ON THE HORIZON

Throughout the latter weeks of the presidential campaign in 2008, the two candidates offered an increasingly costly and often mind-boggling array of proposed new federal programs. At one point, John McCain said, if elected, he would "help out" 3 million Americans who were at risk of losing their homes. McCain also supported more government help for people in paying for health insurance.

Soon-to-be-elected Barack Obama argued in favor of even more new government spending. He said that he would create 2 million new jobs by rebuilding our crumbling infrastructure and "laying broadband lines that reach every corner of the country." He promised to spend $15 billion a year over the next ten years on renewable energy. He had a plan to "make health care affordable and accessible for every American." He said he would invest in early childhood education and "recruit an army of new teachers." And in an editorial in the *Wall Street Journal* the day before the election, he said that he was willing to make a deal with every young American: "If you commit to serving your community or your country, we will make sure you can afford your tuition."

At the same time that these new government programs were being promised, Congress was separately considering an additional multibillion-dollar "economic stimulus" plan. Moreover, many nongovernment organizations had their own ideas for more federal spending. For example, in November 2008, the Campaign for America's Future organized a convention in which the theme was the creation of a government-funded investment fund for public works projects. Simultaneously, the Center for American Progress released a two-year, $100 billion plan for producing renewable energy. The latter group argued that increased government spending should also go to schools, health care, job training, and technology innovation. Another group, Realizing the Dream, Inc., wanted the federal government to commit the necessary funds to reduce poverty by 50 percent in the next ten years.

Even as the chorus of voices in favor of additional federal government spending on new programs was growing, Secretary of the Treasury Henry Paulson was already doling out the hundreds of billions of dollars authorized under the $700 billion "bailout" bill (officially called the Emergency Economic Stabilization Act of 2008). Almost simultaneously, even more federal spending was being pushed hard by Representative Charles Rangel (D., N.Y.). When asked about the effect these additional programs would have on the deficit, Rangel said that he did not want to hear about that. "For God's sake," he said, "don't ask me where the money will come from. I'm going to the same place Paulson went."

Where is "the same place Paulson went"?

Increased Spending, Increased Taxes

When Congress passes legislation to spend more, whether it is for bailing out the financial sector, improving education and public infrastructure, or attempting to reduce poverty, there is ultimately only one place it can obtain the resources. That place is you and everyone else who earns income each year in the United States. As we noted in Chapters 13 and 14, having the ability to run a larger federal government deficit (and thus increase the net national debt) does not change the fundamental budget constraint facing our society.

What government spends, the rest of us do not spend. Perhaps without your realizing it, your **real tax rate** has already gone up in the last several years. Why? Because federal government spending has increased as a percentage of **gross domestic product (GDP).** Your real tax rate is easily calculated. It is the percentage of GDP controlled by the government. The observed taxes that you pay through automatic withholding of federal income taxes on your wages or salary will eventually catch up. The budget constraint guarantees that.

But What about All Those Tax Credits?

During the heat of the 2008 presidential campaign, Barack Obama said he wanted to give tax relief to 95 percent of all households. Let's look at these numbers. Currently, only about 60 percent of American households pay federal income taxes (down from about 80 percent in 1984). Almost 59 million tax filers do not pay any federal income taxes. So how can the government reduce income taxes for an individual or a household that does not pay any? It can (and does) do this by what is known as a **tax credit,** or a *refundable tax credit,* as it is known at the IRS. Under a tax credit, people who pay no federal income taxes effectively get a check from the federal government, which they can use to pay other federal taxes they might owe (such as Social Security) or to pay *future* federal tax liabilities, should they arise. And if there are no current or likely future tax liabilities, well, they get to keep the cash. Consider some of the proposed tax credits that might already be in place by the time you read this:

- A $500 refund to low- and middle-income workers to offset Social Security taxes
- A tax credit covering 50 percent of child care expenses up to $6,000 a year
- A $4,000 tax credit for college students paying tuition if they perform "community service"

- A refundable 10 percent mortgage-interest tax credit for taxpayers who fill out the simplified tax form (Form 1040A)
- A $3,000 tax credit for businesses that hire new workers in 2009 and 2010

So, you might be asking, if so many Americans are going to get tax credits, what is the basis for our prediction that taxes will nonetheless increase? The answer goes back to the first paragraph of this chapter. No government obtains funding from the moon or from Mars. Every single penny that government spends, someone in the private sector does not spend. We already saw in 2008 and 2009 an increase in federal government spending of trillions of dollars on "bailing out" the economy and "stimulating" the economy. If we add to those expenditures additional ones creating more renewable energy, reducing poverty, subsidizing for college attendance, and more, the share of government spending as a percentage of total annual national spending will continue to rise. Thus total taxes must rise.

If, in addition, 95 percent of taxpayers see "tax relief" as Obama promised during the 2008 campaign, the remaining 5 percent of taxpayers will receive a bill for much more than they are currently paying in federal income taxes. Yet higher taxes on the very richest Americans are not going to be sufficient to pay for all of the increased government spending, especially if other people are getting their taxes cut. The highest 5 percent of income earners in the United States already pay over 60 percent of all federal income taxes. As you will read about in the following chapter, sending them a bill for a larger proportion of a larger total tax bill is likely to cause them to change their behavior in ways that will reduce the growth of total income and possibly even reduce the level of total tax receipts.

IS ARGENTINA SHOWING THE WAY?

Argentina was one of the ten richest countries in the world a hundred years ago. It has since slipped to about seventieth on that list. Over the same period of time, government spending (and taxes) in Argentina has been growing relative to the overall size of the economy. Most recently, Argentine president Cristina Kirchner announced that the nation's private pension system was being taken over by the national government. While she claimed that it was for the "good of the people," because the market was too risky for retirement savings, in fact President Kirchner wanted to use those assets to fund more government spending. Technically, the government will "borrow" from the retirement system. But because the Argentine government has a track record of defaulting on its borrowings, many people expect that they will get back few, if any, of their hard-earned retirement pesos.

As you might expect, contributions into the private pension plan plummeted as soon as the government announced its plan. Some Argentine citizens quietly began moving other **assets** out of the country, hoping to protect them from similar confiscation. Still others began making plans for moving *themselves* out of the country, on the grounds that emigration was the ultimate form of protection.

The Argentine government's nationalization of the private pension system is simply a once-and-for-all increase in taxes. While it is unlikely that the U.S. government would seek to take control of private pension plans here, the Argentine story illustrates the key point of this chapter. What the government spends, we must pay for. Sometimes the government must be creative in making that happen, but happen it will. Hence our prediction: Higher taxes are in your future.

FOR CRITICAL ANALYSIS

1. The government now owns shares of stock and warrants in many banks, insurance companies, some auto companies, and in other sectors of the economy. (Warrants are rights to own future shares of stock.) If the value of the shares owned by the federal government increases because the market price per share rises, in what way could this increase actually permit a reduction in future taxes? Explain.

2. If you are a lower-income-earning individual and receive enough tax credits so that you pay no income taxes, should you care about tax increases for other individuals? Explain.

3. Is it *possible* that in, say, ten years, the real tax rate paid by U.S. residents will be lower than it is today? What circumstances would have to change to make this occur? Explain.

CHAPTER 16

Soak the Rich

"The art of taxation consists in so plucking the goose as to obtain the greatest possible amount of feathers with the smallest possible amount of hissing." So said Jean-Baptiste Colbert (1619–1683), minister of finance under French King Louis XIV. About three hundred years later, the thirty-fifth president of the United States, John F. Kennedy, said, "An economy hampered by restrictive taxes will never produce enough revenue to balance our budget, just as it will never produce enough jobs or enough profits."

Although Colbert and Kennedy both recognized the costs of taxation, they were focused on two very different kinds of costs. Colbert sought to minimize political opposition to taxes he proposed. Kennedy was interested in reducing the *economic* costs of taxes, which arise because higher taxes induce people to produce less output. At various times in America's history, the politicians in power have sometimes taken the Colbert approach to taxation and at other times the Kennedy approach. Most recently, in both Europe and America, politicians have argued that we should "make the rich pay their 'fair' share." Before we can establish whether the rich do or do not pay their fair share of taxes, we must first examine the different types of taxing systems. We can then also get some notion of whether an effort to concentrate taxes on a narrow segment of the population (the "rich") is more in the spirit of Colbert or of Kennedy.

PROPORTIONAL, REGRESSIVE, AND PROGRESSIVE TAXATION SYSTEMS

A **proportional tax system** is the easiest to understand. If the income **tax rate** is, say, 20 percent, every taxable dollar earned is taxed at 20 percent. If you have taxable income of $50,000 a year, you pay $10,000 in income taxes. If you have taxable income of $1 million a year, you pay $200,000 in income taxes.

A **regressive tax system** involves collecting a smaller percentage of taxes as one's income rises. Suppose you are taxed 18 percent on the first $100,000 and 3 percent on everything thereafter. If you make $100,000, you pay $18,000 in income taxes. If you make $200,000, you pay $21,000 in income taxes ($18,000 on the first $100,000 plus $3,000 on the next $100,000).

Many economists argue that sales taxes on food are regressive. Why? Because everyone pays the same percentage tax on food, but higher-income-earning people spend a smaller *share* of their incomes on food. Therefore, the effective average tax rate (taxes divided by income) for food is lower for higher-income-earning individuals.

With a **progressive tax system,** the more you earn, the higher your **marginal tax rate.** Suppose you are taxed 20 percent on the first $50,000 and 30 percent on the next $50,000. If you make $50,000, you will pay $10,000 in taxes. If you make $100,000, you will pay $25,000 in taxes ($10,000 on the first $50,000 plus $15,000 on the next $50,000). Thus the proportion of your income that goes to taxes rises as your income rises.

Notice one important fact: *No matter what taxation system is in place, the more income you make, the more you pay in taxes.* What is at issue in the distinction between tax systems is the size of the *additional* income taxes you pay as your income rises. If the percentage stays the same, we have a proportional tax system; if the percentage drops, we have a regressive tax system. Finally, if the percentage increases, we have a progressive tax system. But whatever the system, as long as the tax rate is positive, the higher your income, the higher your taxes. If you have ever earned a paycheck, this is presumably a lesson you already have seen in action.

Do the Rich Pay More?

The Internal Revenue Service (IRS) keeps extensive data on how much different groups pay in income taxes. In 1979, the IRS started looking at what share of the nation's tax bill the most affluent individuals paid. In that year, the top 1 percent of income earners made 9.3 percent of the nation's income but paid 18.3 percent of its income taxes. At the time, the highest-income-earning U.S. residents were in the 70 percent **tax bracket**—that is, their marginal tax rate was 70 cents on the dollar.

Flash forward to current times. Based on IRS data published in 2007, the top marginal tax rate for the big income earners was about 35 percent.

Table 16–1 Shares of Income and Taxes Paid for Top Earners

Share of Earners	Share of Income	Share of Federal Income Taxes
Top 1%	19%	37%
Top 5%	33%	57%
Top 10%	44%	68%
Top 25%	66%	85%

The top 1 percent of income earners made almost 19 percent of the nation's total annual income. But their share of total federal personal income taxes paid was 37 percent. That's not a typo—the top 1 percent of income-earning U.S. residents paid more than *one-third* of all federal personal income taxes in the United States. The fact that high-income individuals pay a large proportion of U.S. federal personal income taxes is reflected also in Table 16–1. In fact, if we look at those people whose income put them in the top 40 percent of all income earners, we see that they paid 99.1 percent of all federal personal income taxes. And what about the tax burden on the other 60 percent of the people? They paid less than 1 percent of federal income taxes.

Other numbers reveal the same pattern. Over the past few years, the richest 1.3 million tax filers, those with adjusted gross incomes of more than $365,000, paid more federal income taxes than all of the 66 million U.S. filers below the **median income** in the United States—to the tune of *ten times* more.

No matter how you wish to analyze the federal personal income tax system in the United States, there is no doubt that it is highly progressive. You may have read or heard about a rich person somehow avoiding taxes, and that surely does happen. But as a group, the highest-income-earning U.S. residents pay the bulk of federal personal income taxes.

THE FEW PAYING FOR THE MANY

What has been happening over the past several decades is rarely discussed on the TV news or during political debates: A shrinking number of Americans are bearing a larger and larger share of the nation's income tax burden. The flip side of the coin is that a growing share of U.S. residents pay little or no taxes whatsoever. If, when you fill out your federal tax return, you owe *any* income tax, you are still in the majority—but not by much. At least 44 million U.S. resident adults pay *no* federal income taxes (including Social Security taxes).

By the time you read this, many of the **tax rebate** proposals discussed by politicians in 2008 and 2009 may have turned into law. If so, then just about half of all adult Americans will be paying no federal personal income taxes. Consider also that an increasingly large number of Americans actually receive more income through the federal income tax system than they pay. Specifically, about 25 million families and individuals with incomes less than about $40,000 now receive payments through their tax filing as part of the **earned income tax credit** program: They pay *negative* **taxes.**

TAX RATE CUTS FOR THE RICH

Whenever there have been tax rate cuts, the charge has been heard that these were "tax cuts for the rich." That charge, of course, *must* be true. Because the highest-income individuals pay most of the federal income taxes, any effective tax rate cut will benefit them. We could eliminate all of the federal personal income taxes assessed on the bottom 50 percent of income earners in the United States and the U.S. Treasury would see almost no change in total tax revenues received.

We see similar phenomena everywhere in our lives. For example, a small percentage of drivers (such as long-haul truckers and people who commute long distances to work) consume a disproportionately large amount of the gasoline and diesel fuel used in America. When the price of fuel falls, most of the savings go to these truckers and commuters. The little old lady who drives only to church on Sunday saves almost nothing. To complain that tax cuts benefit the rich is roughly equivalent to complaining that most of the benefits of lower fuel prices are enjoyed by the people who drive the most.

WHO ARE THE RICH?

Although **wealth** is obviously passed down from one generation to another, when we look at the **standard of living** of individuals, very little of that standard of living is determined by the financial inheritance they received from their ancestors. Instead, current living standards of people are chiefly determined by the incomes they have earned for themselves. Moreover, these incomes are chiefly the result of what they have produced in the workplace.[1]

---

1. We do inherit plenty of nonfinancial wealth from our parents, of course, including intelligence and work habits, which do play a role in determining how much we produce and hence our standard of living.

Given the great disparities in income across people, this may seem strange, but it is easily seen in professional sports. You may have noticed huge disparities in the income received by different athletes, even when they are playing in the same position on the same team. A closer look reveals that these differences are not randomly determined. Instead, more productive players are paid more than less productive ones—lots more. (Tiger Woods doesn't earn $120 million a year just because he went to Stanford.) And although it is easier to see with sports, the link between **productivity** and pay is just as true across all occupations: More productive people are usually paid more.

HOW MARGINAL TAX RATES CHANGE BEHAVIOR

Now, what happens if we decide to "soak the rich" in the sports world? That is, suppose we decided to reduce the salaries of the most productive athletes and hand it out to the least productive. Economics predicts that overall performance would suffer. Athletes would spend less time working out in the off-season; they would spend less time practicing year round; they would devote less effort to studying their opponents— the list goes on and on. And the result would be a decline in the quality of the competition and less enjoyment for fans: Output, no matter how we measure it, would fall. To be sure, many players would still be motivated by pride and inherent competitive drive, but the extra edge offered by financial rewards would be gone—and so would the performance edge.

The same sorts of incentives are established when we use taxes to "soak the rich." As long as incomes are determined chiefly by performance (and the evidence is that they are), higher marginal tax rates on high-income earners are equivalent to higher tax rates on the most productive people. As in sports, the result is reduced performance and lower output. And this is not hypothetical, as revealed by the converse: Tax rate *cuts* lead to more work effort and more output—as occurred in the 1960s, the 1980s, and the early 2000s.

Does this mean that highly progressive tax systems are "good" or "bad"? That we cannot answer, for it entails a value judgment on which economics offers no guidance. What we can say is that taxes discourage production, and the higher the tax rate, the greater the discouragement. This is the cost of taxes that concerned John Kennedy. In contrast, when the rich are in the minority, soaking the rich can generate a lot of tax dollars with hissing by relatively few people. And this was exactly the point made by Jean-Baptiste Colbert so long ago.

FOR CRITICAL ANALYSIS

1. President Obama campaigned on the theme that he was going to reduce taxes for 95 percent of working Americans. Why would such a campaign promise be difficult to put into practice?

2. Some countries, particularly in Europe, have imposed a **wealth tax.** It is typically based on everything a person owns minus everything the person owes (the difference between what is owned and what is owed is called **net worth**). Put yourself in the shoes of an individual in a country that has just decided to impose a wealth tax. How does a wealth tax affect your incentive to accumulate wealth? How does it affect your incentive to work hard?

3. Explain why individuals and businesses respond more to changes in marginal tax rates than to changes in **average tax rates.**

CHAPTER 17

The Myths of Social Security

You have probably heard politicians debate the need to reform Social Security. If you are under the age of thirty, this debate has been going on for your entire lifetime. Why has nothing been done? The reason is that the politicians are debating over "facts" that are not facts: Most of the claims made about Social Security are myths—urban legends, if you like. Sadly, the politicians have been repeating these myths so often for so long that they believe them, and so do their constituents (perhaps including you). As long as these myths persist, nothing meaningful will be done about Social Security, and the problem will simply get worse. So let's see if we can't cut through the fog by examining some of the worst Social Security myths.

MYTH 1: THE ELDERLY ARE POOR

The Social Security Act was passed in 1935 as the United States was emerging from the Great Depression. The **unemployment rate** at the time was the highest in our nation's history. **Bank runs** and the stock market crash of 1929 had wiped out the savings of millions of people. Many elderly people had little or no **resources** to draw on in retirement, and their extended families often had few resources with which to help them. In the midst of these conditions, Social Security was established to make sure that the elderly had access to some *minimum* level of income when they retired. It was never meant to be the sole source of retirement funds for senior citizens.

Given the circumstances of the program's founding, it is not surprising that many people associate Social Security with poverty among the elderly. The fact is that both the Social Security program and the financial condition of older people have changed dramatically over the years. For example, measured in today's dollars, initial Social Security payments were as little as $110 per month and reached a maximum of $450 per month, or about $5,400 per year. Today, however, many recipients are eligible for payments well in excess of $25,000 per year. More important, people over age sixty-five are no longer among the poorest in our society.

Despite the ravages of the recession of 2007–2009, today's elderly have accumulated literally *trillions* of dollars in **assets.** These assets include homes that are fully paid for and substantial portfolios of stocks and **bonds.** In addition, millions of older Americans are drawing *private* pensions, built up over years of employment. Social Security payments, for example, now provide only about 40 percent of the income of the average retired person, with the rest coming about equally from private pensions, employment earnings, and investment income. Far from being the age group with the highest poverty rate, the elderly actually suffer about 25 percent *less* poverty than the average of all U.S. residents. To be sure, Social Security helps make this possible, but just as surely, only about 10 percent of the elderly are living in poverty. In contrast, the poverty rate among children is twice as high as it is among people over age sixty-five.

MYTH 2: SOCIAL SECURITY IS FIXED INCOME

Most economic and political commentators and laypersons alike treat Social Security benefits as a source of fixed income for the elderly, one that supposedly falls in **real purchasing power** as the general **price level** rises. This myth, too, has its roots in the early days of Social Security, when payments were indeed fixed in dollar terms and thus were subject to the ravages of **inflation.** But this is no longer true. In 1972, Congress decided to link Social Security payments to a measure of the overall price level in the economy. The avowed reason for this change was to protect Social Security payments from any decline in real value during inflation. In fact, because of the price level measure chosen by Congress, the real value of payments actually rises when there is inflation.

Although there are many potential measures of the average price of goods and services, Congress decided to tie Social Security payments to the **consumer price index (CPI).** The CPI is supposed to measure changes in the dollar cost of consuming a bundle of goods and services that is representative for the typical consumer. Thus a 10 percent rise in the CPI is supposed to mean that the **cost of living** has gone up by 10 percent. Accordingly, the law provides that Social Security benefits are automatically increased by 10 percent.

As it turns out, however, the CPI actually overstates the true inflation rate: It is *biased upward* as a measure of inflation. This bias has several sources. For example, when the price of a good rises relative to other prices, people usually consume less of it, enabling them to avoid some of the added cost of the good. But the CPI does not take this into account. Similarly, although the average quality of goods and services generally rises over time, the CPI does not adequately account for this fact. Overall, it has been estimated that until recently, the upward bias in the CPI amounted to about 1.1 percentage points per year on average. Revisions to the CPI have reduced this bias to about 0.8 percent per year. Thus currently, if the CPI says prices have gone up, say, 1.8 percent, they've really gone up only 1.0 percent. Nevertheless, Social Security payments are automatically increased by the full 1.8 percent.

Now, 0.8 or 1.1 percentage points don't sound like much. And if it happened only once or twice, there wouldn't be much of a problem. But almost every year for nearly forty years, this extra amount has been added to benefits. And over a long time, even the small upward bias begins to amount to a real change in **purchasing power.** Indeed, this provision of the Social Security system has had the cumulative effect of raising real (inflation-adjusted) Social Security benefits by almost 50 percent over this period. So despite the myth that Social Security is fixed income, in reality the benefits grow even faster than inflation.

MYTH 3: THERE IS A SOCIAL SECURITY TRUST FUND

For the first few years of Social Security's existence, taxes were collected but no benefits were paid. The funds collected were used to purchase U.S. Treasury bonds, and that accumulation of bonds was called the Social Security Trust Fund. Even today, tax collections (called **payroll taxes**) exceed benefits paid each year—currently by more than $150 billion per year—so that the trust fund now has well over $2 *trillion* in Treasury bonds on its books. Eventually, after the fund reaches a peak of around $2.6 trillion, retiring baby boomers will drive outgoing benefits above incoming tax collections. The bonds will be sold to finance the difference; by around 2040, all of them will be sold, and thereafter all benefits in excess of payroll taxes will have to be financed explicitly out of current taxes.

The standard story told (by politicians at least) is that the bonds in the trust fund represent net assets, much like the assets owned by private pension plans. This is false. Congress has already spent the past excess of taxes over benefits and has simply given the trust fund IOUs. These IOUs are called U.S. Treasury bonds, and they are nothing more than promises by the U.S. Treasury to levy taxes on someone to pay benefits. When it is time for the trust fund to redeem the IOUs it holds, Congress will have to raise taxes, cut spending on other programs, or borrow more to raise the funds. But this would be true even if there were *no* Treasury bonds in the trust fund: All Social Security benefits must ultimately be paid for out of taxes. So whatever might have been intended for the trust fund, the only asset actually backing that fund is nothing more and nothing less than an obligation of Americans—you—to pay taxes in the future.

MYTH 4: SOCIAL SECURITY WILL BE THERE FOR YOU

Social Security was a great deal for Ida Mae Fuller, who in 1940 became the first person to receive a regular Social Security pension. She had paid a total of $25 in Social Security taxes before she retired. By the time she died in 1975 at the age of one hundred, she had received benefits totaling $23,000. And although Ida Mae did better than most recipients, the *average* annual real rate of return for those early retirees was an astounding 135 percent *per year.* (That is, after adjusting for inflation, every initial $100 in taxes paid yielded $135 *per year* during each and every year of that person's retirement.)

People retiring more recently have not done quite so well, but everyone who retired by about 1970 has received a far better return from Social Security than could likely have been obtained from any other investment. These higher benefits relative to contributions were made possible because *at each point in time, current retirees are paid benefits out of the taxes paid by individuals who are currently working.* Social Security is a **pay-as-you-go system;** it is not like a true retirement plan in which participants pay into a fund and receive benefits according to what they have paid in and how much that fund has cumulatively earned. So as long as Social Security was pulling in enough new people each year, the system could offer benefits that were high relative to taxes paid. But the number of people paying Social Security taxes is no longer growing so fast, and the number of retirees is growing faster. Moreover, today's trickle of new retirees is becoming tomorrow's flood as the baby boom generation exits the workforce. The result is bad news all around.

One way to think about the problem facing us—which is chiefly a problem facing *you*—is to contemplate the number of retirees each worker must support. In 1945, forty-two workers shared the burden of each Social Security recipient. By 1960, nine workers had to pick up the tab for each person collecting Social Security. Today, the burden of a retiree is spread out among slightly more than four workers. By 2030 or so, fewer than three workers will be available to pay the Social Security benefits due each recipient.

The coming tax bill for all of this will be staggering. If we *immediately* raised Social Security (payroll) taxes from 15.3 percent to a bit over 19 percent—more than a 24 percent increase—and kept them there for the next seventy-five years or so, the system's revenues would probably be large enough to meet its obligations. But this would be the largest tax increase in U.S. history, which makes it extremely unlikely that it will occur. Yet every day that Congress delays, the situation gets worse. If Congress waits until 2030 to raise taxes, they will have to be increased by more than 50 percent. Indeed, some commentators are predicting that without fundamental reforms to the system, payroll taxes *alone* will have to be hiked to 25 percent of wages—in addition to regular federal, state, and local income taxes, of course.

And what form are these reforms likely to take? Well, rules will specify that people must be older before they become eligible for Social Security benefits. Existing legislation has already scheduled a hike in the age for full benefits up to sixty-seven from its current sixty-six. Almost certainly, this age threshold will be raised again, perhaps to seventy. Moreover, it is likely that all Social Security benefits (rather than just a portion) will eventually be subject to federal income taxes. It is even possible that some high-income individuals—you, perhaps—will be declared ineligible for benefits because their income from other sources is too high.

So what does all this mean for you? Well, technically, a Social Security system will probably be in existence when you retire, although the retirement age will be higher than today and benefits will have been scaled back significantly. It is also likely that, strictly speaking, the Social Security Trust Fund will still be around when you hit the minimum age for benefits. But whatever else happens to the Social Security system between now and your retirement, you can be secure in your knowledge of one thing: You will be getting a much bigger tax bill from the federal government to pay for it.

For Critical Analysis

1. Where has all of the Social Security money gone?

2. People over the age of sixty-five have been highly successful in protecting and enhancing the real benefits they receive from Social Security. This has come at the expense of other people in society, particularly young people. What do you think explains the ability of older people to win political battles with younger people?

3. Analyze how each of the following hypothetical policy changes would affect people's decision to retire. Would the change induce people to retire sooner or later? Explain your reasoning.

(a) An increase in the age at which one can receive full Social Security benefits (currently age sixty-six to sixty-seven, depending on the year in which a person was born)

(b) A decrease in the fraction (currently 70 percent) of full benefits that one can receive if retirement occurs at age sixty-two

(c) An increase in the Medicare eligibility age from its current level of sixty-five

(d) An increase to 100 percent from its current 85 percent in the maximum fraction of Social Security benefits that is subject to the federal income tax

CHAPTER 18

The Hazards of High Taxes

Politicians always seem to be looking for additional ways to raise tax revenues. And most often, politicians talk (and even act) as though their taxing decisions have no effect on the quantity supplied or the quantity demanded of whatever good or service they wish to tax. Indeed, there is a saying among economists that politicians believe that all demand curves and supply curves are **perfectly inelastic.** In such a world, higher taxes would have no effect on either quantity demanded or quantity supplied. What a wonderful world that would be—at least for politicians. In this chapter, you will see how important **microeconomics** is for understanding what are thought to be macroeconomic issues. Tax policies are often thought of as one of the latter, which they are. But tax policies cannot be understood without putting them in the context of how people respond to them.

THE FAILURE OF LUXURY-GOOD TAXES

In the real world, changes in taxes cause changes in **relative prices,** and individuals in their roles as consumers, savers, investors, and workers do react to these relative price changes. Consider a truly telling example from not so long ago—the luxury tax enacted by Congress in 1991. Members of Congress were looking for additional revenues to reduce the **federal budget deficit.** What better place to find those needed revenues than with new taxes on the purchases of high-priced luxury items, such as big boats, expensive cars, furs, planes, and jewelry? After all, rich people don't really care how much they pay, right? That is why we call them rich. So Congress passed a 10 percent luxury surcharge tax on boats priced over $100,000, cars priced over $30,000, aircraft priced over $250,000, and furs and jewelry priced over $10,000.

The federal government estimated that it would rake in $9 billion in extra tax revenues over the following five-year period. Yet just a few years later, the luxury boat tax was quietly eliminated. The luxury car tax was also dropped, as were those special taxes imposed on furs, aircraft, and jewelry. Why? Because the actual take for the federal government was almost *nothing*.

Rich people, it turns out, react to relative price changes just like everyone else. Instead of buying high-priced new boats, for example, they found alternatives. Some purchased used luxury boats instead of new ones. Others decided not to trade in their older boats for new ones. Still others bought their new boats in other countries and never brought them back to the United States to be taxed. Similar changes in behavior occurred in the markets for other luxury goods. The moral of the story for politicians is that the laws of **supply** and **demand** apply to everyone, rich and poor, young and old.

STATIC VERSUS DYNAMIC ANALYSIS

The discrepancy between the fantasyland of many politicians and the reality of human behavior can be traced in part to the fact that politicians routinely engage in what is called **static economic analysis.** They assume that people's behavior is static (unchanging), no matter how the constraints they face—such as higher taxes—might change. If the politicians who had pushed for the luxury tax had used **dynamic economic analysis,** they would have correctly anticipated that consumers (even rich ones) were going to change their buying decisions when faced with the new taxes.

Dynamic analysis takes into account the fact that the impact of the **tax rate** on tax revenues actually collected depends crucially on the **elasticity** of the relevant demand or supply curves. That is, even a high *rate* (measured in tax per item or as a percentage of the value of the item) can yield relatively little *revenue* (total dollars collected) if consumers are highly responsive to the tax-inclusive price of the good. For example, in the case of the luxury tax, the elasticity of demand for new, high-end boats was relatively high: When the tax per boat went up, the quantity demanded fell so far that tax collections were negligible.

RESPONDING TO HIGHER FEDERAL MARGINAL INCOME TAX RATES

Now let's shift from the demand side of this taxing issue to the supply side. Does quantity supplied react to changing relative prices? Yes, but you might not know it from listening to members of Congress (and even some presidents). The first modern federal personal income tax was imposed in 1916. The highest rate was 15 percent. Eventually, the top federal personal marginal income tax rate reached an astounding 91 percent, during the years 1951 to 1964. This **marginal tax rate** dropped to 70 percent in 1965. In 1980, it was lowered to 50 percent. For much of the 1980s and since, the highest federal marginal income tax rate has ranged from 31 percent to just under 40 percent.

Often politicians (and even some members of the general public) believe that the income tax rates paid by America's richest individuals do not matter to them because they are so rich that even after paying taxes, they are still very rich. The underlying "theory" behind such a belief is that the supply of labor is completely unresponsive to the net, after-tax price received by the providers of labor. Stated another way, if you were to draw the supply curve of labor, it would be a nearly vertical line for each individual at some fixed number of work hours per year; supposedly, the elasticity of supply of labor is low.

To be sure, you might know somebody who loves work so much that she or he will work with the same intensity and quality and for the same number of hours per year no matter what the income tax rate is. But changes occur at the margin in economics (meaning in the real world). If there are *some* individuals who respond to higher federal marginal tax rates by working less, the overall supply curve of labor is going to be upward-sloping even for the ultra-rich—just like all other supply curves for goods and services.

The data seem to confirm our economic predictions. In 1980, the top marginal income tax rate was 70 percent. The highest 1 percent of income-earning Americans paid 19 percent of all federal personal income taxes in that year. In 2007, when the top tax rate was 35 percent, the richest 1 percent paid roughly double that share. How can this be explained? The answer is relatively straightforward: Lower marginal federal personal income tax rates create an incentive for people to work more and harder, because the rewards of doing so are greater. Also, in their role as risk-taking entrepreneurs, individuals are almost always going to be willing to take bigger risks if they know that success will yield greater net after-tax increases in their incomes.

Responding to Incentives

Data from Europe suggest that exactly the same incentives are at work across a broad spectrum of income earners. Researchers have found that a tax increase of just over 12 percentage points induces the average adult in Europe to reduce work effort by over 120 hours per year—the equivalent of almost four weeks' work. Such a tax change also causes a sharp reduction in the number of people who work at all and causes many others to join the **underground economy,** where no income is taxed. Overall, then, higher tax rates cause lower output and higher unemployment and also induce marked increases in efforts devoted to **tax evasion.**

It is also true that what we have been talking about applies even among people who are at the very bottom of the income distribution. In many countries today, and in many circumstances in the United States, poorer individuals receive benefits from the government. These benefits can be in the form of food stamps, subsidized housing, subsidized health care or health insurance, and direct cash payments (often referred to as "welfare"). Those who receive such government benefits typically pay no income taxes on these benefits. In the case of the United States, they may even receive an **earned income tax credit,** which is a type of **negative tax** or **tax credit.**

If such individuals accept a job (or a higher-paying job, if already employed), two things will normally occur. The first is that they will lose some or all of their government benefits. The second is that they may have to start paying federal (and perhaps state) personal income taxes. They understand that the loss of a benefit is the equivalent of being taxed more. And when they also have to pay explicit taxes, they know that the result is effectively double taxation.

Just as at the top end of the income ladder, the quantity of labor supplied by people at the lower end is affected by changes in the marginal income tax rates they face. If taking a good job and getting off the welfare rolls means losing benefits plus paying income taxes, the person on welfare has less incentive to accept a job.

IRELAND: FROM BASKET CASE TO SUPERSTAR

A good case in point is Ireland, which for most of the past two decades was the fastest-growing economy in all of Europe. Twenty-five years ago, its economy was a disaster, among the poorest of European countries. One of the problems was that people on welfare faced an effective (implicit) marginal income tax rate of about 120 percent if they got off welfare and went back to work. Obviously, they weren't directly taxed at 120 percent, but with the actual income tax that would apply plus the loss in welfare benefits, the implicit marginal tax rate was indeed 120 percent. Stated differently, their available spendable income would drop by about 20 percent if they went back to work! Needless to say, large numbers of poorer Irish stayed on the welfare roles until the program was completely overhauled.

Interestingly, this overhaul of the incentives facing low-income individuals was accompanied by an overhaul of the **tax rates** (and thus incentives) facing high-income corporations, with much the same results. In the 1990s, the Irish slashed the corporate **profits** tax to 12.5 percent, the lowest in Europe and only about one-third as high as the U.S. rate of 35 percent. Beginning in 2004, the Irish government also began offering a 20 percent tax credit for company spending on research and development, offering high-tech firms an opportunity to cut their taxes by starting up and expanding operations in Ireland. Almost immediately, Ireland became a magnet for new investment and for successful companies that didn't want to hand over a third or more of their profits to the tax collector.

The combination of lower corporate tax rates and tax breaks on research and development induced hundreds of multinational corporations to begin operations in Ireland. They brought with them hundreds of thousands of new jobs (and this to a nation of only 4 million residents), and Ireland quickly became number one among the **European Union's** fifteen original members in being home to companies that conduct research and development. And tax revenues of the Irish government? Well, despite the drastic cut in tax rates, tax revenues actually soared to levels never seen before. Indeed, measured as a share of **gross domestic product,** the Irish collected 50 percent *more* tax *revenues* out of corporate profits than America did, despite Ireland's lower tax *rate.*

THE MORAL OF THE STORY

The lesson of our story is simple. It is surely true that "nothing in life is certain but death and taxes." But it is equally true that higher tax rates don't always mean higher tax revenues. And that is a lesson that politicians can ignore only at their own peril.

FOR CRITICAL ANALYSIS

1. If you found yourself in the 91 percent federal personal income tax bracket in 1951, how great would have been your incentive to find legal **loopholes** to reduce your federal tax **liabilities?** If you found yourself in the lowest federal personal income tax bracket of, say, 15 percent, would your incentive to find loopholes to reduce your tax bill have remained the same? Explain.

2. Let's suppose that federal marginal personal income tax rates rise significantly over the next ten years. Explain the ways in which individuals at all levels of income can react over time, not just immediately after taxes are raised. How will the size of the response differ,

say, a year after the rise in tax rates compared to a week after the increase? Is it possible that some people will actually change their behavior *before* the higher tax rates go into effect? Explain.

3. How does the structure of a country's tax system affect who decides to immigrate into the nation or emigrate out of the nation? Contrast, for example, nations A and B. Assume that nation A applies a 20 percent tax rate on every dollar of income earned by an individual. Nation B applies a 10 percent tax rate on the first $40,000 per year of income and a 40 percent tax rate on all income above $40,000 per year earned by an individual. Start by computing the tax bill in each country that must be paid by a person earning $40,000 a year and the tax bill that must be paid by a person earning $100,000 per year. Then consider the more general issue: If the language, culture, and climate of the two nations are similar, and if a person can choose to live on one side or the other of a river separating the two nations, who is more likely to choose to live in A, and who is more likely to choose to live in B? To what extent does your reasoning apply if an ocean, rather than a river, separates the two countries? Does it apply if the language, culture, or climate in the two nations differs? Explain.

PART FOUR

Monetary Policy and Financial Institutions

CHAPTER 19

The Fed and Financial Panics

The Panic of 1907 began after an attempt by Otto Heinze to "corner the market" on **shares of stock** in the United Copper Company. Heinze expected the demand for United's shares to increase in the near term and thought that if he bought up enough shares quickly at low prices, he could turn around and sell them at a handsome **profit.** His judgment proved wrong, and Heinze had to sell out at disastrously low prices. Not only did his stock brokerage firm go out of business as a result; more disastrously, the public's confidence in the financial condition of banks that had large holdings of United Copper shares evaporated. Confidence also plummeted regarding the financial health of several banks with whom Otto's brother Augustus was associated.

All of these banks suffered **bank runs,** in which large numbers of customers simultaneously withdrew their deposits, and some ultimately failed as a result. The banking panic soon spread more widely, threatening the security of the entire financial system. It was eventually halted only when the famed financier J. P. Morgan induced a large number of banks to join a consortium and mutually stand behind each other's financial obligations.

BIRTH OF THE FED

The Panic of 1907 achieved notoriety at the time by causing the recession of 1907–1908, but the panic's longer-term importance lies elsewhere. Hoping to avoid a repeat of 1907's financial meltdown, Congress in 1913 established the **Federal Reserve System,** commonly referred to as **the Fed.** The Fed is now the nation's monetary authority and, among other things, our first line of defense against financial panics.

As it had been in prior financial panics, the crux of many banks' woes in 1907 was their inability to convert their assets into the cash that panicked depositors desperately wanted. So the Fed was created to serve as "lender of last resort" to the nation's **commercial banks.** Congress empowered the Fed to lend funds to banks to meet whatever demands that depositors put on the banks, regardless of how great those demands might be. The intention was that there would never be another financial panic in the United States, an objective that, if achieved, would significantly reduce the number and severity of the nation's economic **recessions.**

OPPORTUNITY AND FAILURE

The Fed's first real chance to perform as lender of last resort—the function for which it was created—came in 1930 when several prominent New York banks got into financial difficulties. Customers of those and other banks started withdrawing funds, fearing that their banks might be weak. This spreading lack of confidence was exactly the scenario the Fed was created to defend against—yet it did nothing. The result was a banking panic and a worsening of the economic downturn already under way.

The next year, the Fed had two more opportunities to act as lender of last resort when confidence in banks sagged, yet in both cases it again failed to act. The results were recurrent bank panics in 1931 and an intensification of what was by then an extremely severe recession. Early in 1933, eroding public confidence in the banking system gave the Fed yet another opportunity to step in as lender of last resort, and *again* it failed to do so. The resulting banking panic was disastrous and ushered in the deepest stages of what has come to be known as the Great Depression. It is little wonder that Herbert Hoover, who was president of the United States at the time, referred to the Fed as "a weak reed for a nation to lean on in time of trouble."

LESSONS LEARNED

Thirty years after the end of the Great Depression, Nobel laureate Milton Friedman and Anna Schwartz published *A Monetary History of the United States.* Among other things, this book laid out in detail the story of the Fed's failings during the 1930s. The book's lessons were absorbed by at least two people who have since served as the head of the Fed— Alan Greenspan, who was chair of the Fed from 1987 to 2006, and Ben Bernanke, who succeeded Greenspan.

Greenspan's opportunity to have the Fed serve as the banking system's lender of last resort came in September 2001, in the wake of the terrorist attacks on the World Trade Center towers. Banks found themselves in need of a quick infusion of funds as panicked depositors made large-scale withdrawals of cash. The Fed quickly stepped in to provide funds to banks, enabling them to meet the demands of depositors without having to sell off **assets** quickly at depressed prices. A terrorist attack had surely never been contemplated by the legislators who created the Fed. Nevertheless, the Fed acted vigorously as a lender of last resort and thus certainly achieved the objectives of its creators: prevention of financial panic.

THE PANIC OF '08

Only two years after he replaced Greenspan as chair of the Fed, Ben Bernanke had an even bigger opportunity to put the Fed to work. Late in 2008, rapidly eroding confidence in America's financial system led to the near or total collapse of several major financial firms. Many commercial banks, investment banks, and even insurance companies were suddenly in dire condition, and potential borrowers across the country found themselves unable to obtain funds from anyone, at any rate of interest. Although circumstances differed from 1907 in that commercial banks were not at the center of the panic, there was no doubt about one point: The Panic of '08 was just as threatening to the U.S. economy as its century-old predecessor had been.

Mindful of the costs of inaction, the Fed moved swiftly to maintain and restore confidence in key components of the financial system. But its actions were considerably broader than ever before. Historically, for example, the Fed has lent funds to commercial banks and to the federal government itself. But in 2008, the Fed also lent hundreds of billions of dollars directly to nonbank corporations around the country, including tens of billions to insurance giant AIG. The Fed also began purchasing obligations of government-sponsored **mortgage** market giants Fannie Mae and Freddie Mac, hoping to encourage more lending for home purchases. And finally, the Fed agreed to the following trade with commercial banks: It would exchange billions of dollars of risk-free federal **bonds** it held for billions of dollars of high-risk private bonds that they held. In effect, the Fed helped the banks remove high-risk assets of questionable value from their **balance sheets,** thus reducing the chances that skittish depositors might suddenly make large-scale withdrawals of funds from commercial banks.

THE SURGE IN EXCESS RESERVES

On many of their deposits, commercial banks are required to keep a minimum amount of **reserves** on hand, either in their vaults or on deposit with the Fed. These are referred to as **required reserves.** Any reserves above these minimum required levels are called **excess reserves.** Over the past seventy years, bank holdings of excess reserves have generally been quite small, amounting to no more than a few billion dollars for the entire banking system. And this is not surprising. In normal times, banks generally keep only enough excess reserves to handle day-to-day transactions with depositors because they can earn interest on any funds they lend out.

By 2009, excess reserves soared to more than $800 billion. Total reserves (required plus excess) were up sharply because the Fed was giving banks reserves in return for other assets. Among the purchases: commercial paper (debts issued by private companies), securities backed by credit-card debt and home mortgages, and even home mortgages themselves. But almost all of these reserves simply sat there—either in bank vaults or on deposit with the Fed—because banks lent almost none of them out.

Banks across the country held on to the excess reserves for three reasons. First, the deteriorating economy meant that borrowers were riskier and hence less profitable at any given interest rate. Second, depositors were growing increasingly concerned about the financial condition of commercial banks. The banks therefore wanted plenty of funds on hand—in the form of excess reserves—in case they had to meet increased withdrawal demands by depositors. Oddly enough, the third reason for the failure of banks to lend out reserves was a new policy implemented by the Fed itself.

PAYING INTEREST ON RESERVES

In 2008, the Fed began paying interest on the reserves held by commercial banks, something it had never done before. And it was paying interest not just on required reserves but on excess reserves as well. This policy encouraged banks to hold excess reserves rather than to lend the funds to customers. Thus the payment of interest on commercial bank reserves made it *more difficult* for companies and individuals to get loans.

On balance, it remains to be seen whether the Fed actions of 2008 lived up to the expectations that the Fed's founders had more than a century ago. By providing funds to banks and other financial institutions, the Fed helped reduce the impact of the financial panic and helped prevent widespread runs on commercial banks. Nevertheless, the Fed decision to pay interest on reserves markedly discouraged banks from lending those reserves to companies and households across the land. Only time and further study will tell whether the Fed's actions prevented the recession of 2007–2009 from becoming one of the worst of the past century.

FOR CRITICAL ANALYSIS

1. How did the Fed's long-standing policy of not paying interest on bank reserves act much like a tax on bank reserves?

2. If the Fed continued to pay interest on required reserves but stopped paying interest on excess reserves, how would bank lending incentives be changed?

3. If the Fed had not injected reserves into the banking system in 2008, what would have been the consequences for the banks and for **aggregate demand?**

CHAPTER 20

Monetary Policy and Interest Rates

"Fed cuts interest rates by half a point." Similar headlines appeared numerous times in the financial press in the first decade of the 2000s. The **Federal Reserve System**—the Fed for short—is America's **central bank.** Interest rates can be affected by the Fed; when they are, that is part of **monetary policy,** defined as the use of changes in the amount of money in circulation to affect interest rates, credit markets, **inflation,** and unemployment.

The theory behind monetary policy is relatively simple. An increase in the **money supply** raises spending on goods and services and thus stimulates the economy, tending to lower unemployment in the short run and raise inflation in the long run. (One important version of the money supply is composed of checking-type account balances and **currency** in the hands of the public.) The flip side is that a decrease in the money supply reduces spending, thereby depressing the economy; the short-run result is higher unemployment, and the long-run effect is a lower inflation rate.

MONETARY POLICY AND THE FED

Congress established the Federal Reserve System in 1913. A board of governors consisting of seven members, including the very powerful chairperson, governs it. All of the governors, including the chair, are nominated by the president and approved by the Senate. Their appointments are for fourteen years (although the chair serves in that role for only four years at a time).

Through the Fed and its Federal Open Market Committee (FOMC), decisions about monetary policy are made eight times a year. The Federal Reserve System is independent; the board even has its own budget, financed with interest earnings on the portfolio of **bonds** it owns. The president can attempt to persuade the board to follow a particular policy, and Congress can threaten to merge the Fed with the Treasury or otherwise restrict its behavior. But unless Congress takes the radical step of passing legislation to the contrary, the Fed's chair and governors can do as they please. Hence talking about "the president's monetary policy" or "Congress's monetary policy" is inaccurate. To be sure, the Fed has, on occasion, yielded to presidential pressure to pursue a particular policy, and the Fed's chair follows a congressional resolution directing him to report on what the Fed is doing on the policy front. But now more than ever before, the Fed remains the single most important and truly independent source of economic power in the federal government. Monetary policy is Fed policy and no one else's.

Federal Reserve monetary policy, in principle, is supposed to be countercyclical. That is, it is supposed to counteract other forces that might be making the economy contract or expand too rapidly. The economy goes through **business cycles,** made up of **recessions** (and sometimes **depressions**) when unemployment is rising and **expansions** when unemployment is falling and businesses are often straining their productive capacity. For the Fed to stabilize the economy, it must implement policies that go counter to business activity. Although Fed policy can be put into place much faster than most federal policies, it still does not operate instantaneously. Indeed, researchers have estimated that it takes almost fourteen months for a change in monetary policy to become effective. Thus by the time monetary policy goes into effect, a different policy might be appropriate.

POLICY IN PRACTICE

Researchers examining the evidence over the period from 1913 to the 1990s have concluded that on average, the Fed's policy has turned out to be procyclical rather than countercyclical. That is, by the time the Fed started pumping money into the economy, it was time to do the opposite, and by the time the Fed started reducing the growth rate of the money supply, it was time to start increasing it. Perhaps the Fed's biggest procyclical blunder occurred during the Great Depression in the 1930s. Many economists believe that what would have been a severe recession turned into the Great Depression because the Fed's actions resulted in an almost one-third decrease in the amount of money in circulation, drastically reducing **aggregate demand.** It has also been argued that the rapid inflation experienced in the 1970s was largely the result of excessive monetary expansion by the Fed.

In the 1990s, few commentators were able to complain about monetary policy. Inflation almost disappeared by the end of the decade, which also saw the **unemployment rate** drop to its lowest level in nearly forty years. Why the Fed was successful in the 1990s remains unclear. It could have been due to the uniquely superior insights of its chair during this period, Alan Greenspan. Or perhaps the Fed had learned from its past experiences. Or it may simply have been a run of good luck. But whatever the reason, it is clear that the Fed remains far from perfect. Late in the decade, it tightened monetary policy sharply, reducing monetary growth and thereby contributing to the recession of 2001.

In 2001 and 2002, the Fed moved to increase the money supply more rapidly, which in turn helped produce economic expansion but also caused the inflation rate to double between 2002 and 2005. The Fed responded to the higher inflation by cutting monetary growth over the period 2004–2006, and by late 2007, we had another recession on our hands. This led the Fed to change gears again, cutting interest rates in 2007 and especially in 2008 as the recession deepened. By the time you read this, our forecast is that the Fed will have altered policy once more.

INFLATION AND INTEREST RATES

Most newspaper discussions of Fed policy focus on its decisions to raise or lower interest rates. Before we can make any sense out of such discussions, we need first to understand the relationship between **nominal interest rates,** which are the rates that you see in the newspaper and pay for loans, and the **expected rate of inflation.**

Let's start in a hypothetical world where there is no inflation, so expected (or anticipated) inflation is zero. In that world, you might be able to borrow—obtain a **mortgage** to buy a home, for example—at a nominal rate of interest of, say, 4 percent. If you borrow the funds and your anticipation of zero inflation turns out to be accurate, neither you nor the lender will have been fooled. The dollars you pay back in the years to come will be just as valuable in terms of **purchasing power** as the dollars that you borrowed. In this situation, we would say that the **real interest rate** (equal to the nominal interest rate minus the expected rate of inflation) was exactly equal to the nominal interest rate.

Contrast this with a situation in which the expected inflation rate is, say, 5 percent. Although you would be delighted to borrow at a 4 percent interest rate, lenders would be reluctant to oblige you, and their reluctance would be based on exactly the same reasoning you would be using: The dollars with which you would be repaying the debt would be declining in purchasing power every year. Lenders would likely insist on (and you would agree to) an **inflationary premium** of 5 percent to make up for the expected inflation. The nominal interest rate would rise to about 9 percent, keeping the real rate at its previous level of 4 percent.

There is strong evidence that inflation rates and nominal interest rates move in parallel. During periods of rapid inflation, people come to anticipate that inflation rather quickly, and higher nominal interest rates are the result. In the early 1970s, when the inflation rate was between 4 and 5 percent, nominal interest rates on mortgages were around 8 to 10 percent. At the beginning of the 1980s, when the inflation rate was near 10 percent, nominal interest rates on mortgages had risen to between 14 and 16 percent. By the middle of the 1990s, when the inflation rate was 2 to 3 percent, nominal interest rates had fallen to between 6 and 8 percent.

POLICY AND INTEREST RATES

Now let's go back to Fed policy and the headlines. When the chair of the Fed states that the Fed is dropping "the interest rate" from, say, 1.5 percent to 1 percent, he really means something else. In the first place, the interest rate referred to is the **federal funds rate,** the rate at which banks can borrow **excess reserves** from other banks. Any effects of Fed policy here will show up in other rates only indirectly. More important, when the Fed decides to try to alter the federal funds rate, it can do so only by actively entering the market for federal government securities (usually Treasury bills). So if the Fed wants to lower "the interest rate," it essentially must buy Treasury bills from banks and other private holders of the bills. This action bids up the prices of these bills and simultaneously lowers the interest rates on them. This in turn lowers the interest rates at which banks are willing to lend to each other and to the public. (In terms of our earlier discussion, this policy also has the effect of increasing the money supply and so increases spending throughout the economy.) Conversely, when the Fed wants to increase "the interest rate," it *sells* Treasury bills, driving their prices down and pushing up interest rates. The result is a reduction in the money supply and a reduction in spending throughout the economy. A Fed declaration that interest rates are going to be changed simply serves to alert people that a new policy is on the way.

The other key point to note is that the changes in interest rates we have been talking about are strictly short-term changes, occurring over a period of time so short that the expected inflation rate is constant. Once the effects of the Fed's new policy begin to kick in, however, the expected inflation rate will tend to respond, which can create a whole new set of problems. For example, suppose the Fed decides to "lower interest rates," that is, to increase the money supply by buying Treasury bills. In the early weeks and months, this will indeed lower interest rates and stimulate spending. But for a given level of productive capacity in the economy, this added spending will eventually be translated into a higher inflation rate. This will soon cause nominal interest rates to *rise* as inflationary expectations get added onto the real interest rate.

The fact of the matter is that although the Fed can cause interest rates to move up or down in the short run via its choice of monetary policy, forces beyond its control determine what interest rates will be in the long run. The real rate is determined by the underlying **productivity** of the economy and the **consumption** preferences of individuals, and the expected inflation rate is determined by people's beliefs about future policy. So when you read that the chair of the Fed has lowered "the interest rate," you know that the growth of the money supply has been increased. But you also now know that whether the Fed likes it or not, if this policy persists long enough, the eventual result will be more inflation in the future and higher, not lower, interest rates.

FOR CRITICAL ANALYSIS

1. Why do you suppose the Fed likes to signal its intentions about monetary policy ahead of time?

2. Some economists have argued that the Fed should stick to a simple monetary rule, such as a stable growth rate of the money supply, regardless of what is going on in the economy. In light of the Fed's performance history, can you suggest why we might benefit from such a rule? Why do you think the Fed has steadfastly refused to implement such a rule?

3. In response to the Panic of '08, the Fed took unprecedented steps to increase the money supply. For example, for the first time ever, it made large-scale acquisitions of commercial paper (indebtedness of private companies), in addition to buying Treasury bonds. At the time, the stock market was falling and unemployment was rising. What do you predict would have happened to both, and to interest rates, if the Fed had not undertaken expansionary monetary policy at this time?

CHAPTER 21

Credit Chaos

The **recession** of 2007–2009 had its origins as far back as 2006. That's when housing prices across the country first began to turn down, leading to widespread **foreclosures** on home **mortgages** and **defaults** on the securities backed by those mortgages. These defaults brought on the collapse of some of the world's largest financial companies and effectively shut down credit markets around the world. The credit collapse caused a massive reduction in business spending, at the same time that falling house prices forced frightened consumers to slash their own spending. By 2008, this one-two punch of lower **investment** and reduced **consumption** had pushed the economy into full-scale recession. But we are getting ahead of ourselves, so let's go back in time just a bit.

HOUSING MARKET ROLLER COASTER

Between 1995 and 2009, the U.S. housing market went on the wildest ride in its history. Over the years 1995 to 2005, median real (inflation-adjusted) house prices soared 60 percent nationwide and then promptly crashed, falling 40 percent in just four years. Over the same period, the proportion of Americans who owned homes, normally a variable that changes quite slowly, leapt from 64 percent to 69 percent and then quickly dropped back to 66 percent. Meanwhile, the number of new houses built each year soared from 1.4 million to 2 million and then plunged to 500,000 per year.

But what really got people's attention—and created huge pressures on financial markets here and abroad—was the fact that just as quickly as people had snapped up houses during the boom years of 1995–2005, they simply *abandoned* their houses beginning in 2006, refusing to make any more payments on their mortgages. In a typical year, about 0.3 percent of homeowners (fewer than one out of three hundred) stop making mortgage payments and thus have their houses go into foreclosure, a process in which the borrower must give up any **equity** (ownership) in a home because of a failure to meet payment obligations. The foreclosure rate doubled to 0.6 percent in 2006, doubled again in 2007, and rose yet again in 2008 and 2009. In some hard-hit states, such as Nevada, foreclosures exploded to more than *ten times* the normal nationwide rate, with one home out of thirty going into foreclosure each year.

Across the country, people were literally walking away from their homes, leaving them in the hands of banks and other lenders. These lenders then took huge financial losses when forced to sell the abandoned properties in a market in which house prices were already falling. The result was further downward pressure on prices, which gave more owners the incentive to walk away from their homes, which raised foreclosures, and so forth. Within just a few years, the housing market was more depressed than it had been at any time since the Great Depression of the 1930s.

What happened? Specifically, we want to know why over this fifteen-year period, the housing market first exploded and then imploded, creating financial chaos on a worldwide scale. Although numerous factors no doubt played a role, there is just as little doubt that the principal culprit was none other than our own Congress. Operating under a banner promoting "affordable housing," Congress first amended key mortgage-lending legislation and then put considerable implicit and explicit pressure on two crucial government-sponsored mortgage agencies. Together, these actions caused mortgage lenders to dramatically reduce the financial standards expected of home-buyers who wished to obtain a mortgage. These lower standards enabled many more people to qualify for mortgages, increasing the demand for housing and leading to the housing boom of 1995–2005. But these same lower standards meant that people in weaker financial condition were heavily represented among new home buyers, which in turn played a central role in creating the housing crash and mortgage meltdown of 2006–2009. To see how this evolved, we are going to have to do some digging in the history books.

SOME HOUSING HISTORY

Prior to World War II, most home mortgages were of short duration, such as a year or two (as opposed to fifteen to thirty years, which is common now). During the Great Depression, many risk-weary lenders refused to renew mortgages when they came due. The state of the economy was such that most borrowers were unable to repay immediately, and so their homes were foreclosed. In response, the U.S. government in 1934 created the Federal Housing Administration (FHA), to guarantee some home mortgages from default, and in 1938 created the Federal National Mortgage Association (FNMA, known as Fannie Mae), to purchase mortgages from the FHA, enabling the latter to guarantee still more mortgages. In 1968, Congress authorized Fannie Mae to buy mortgages from virtually all lenders, and in 1970, Congress created Freddie Mac (the Federal Home Mortgage Loan Corporation) to offer competition to Fannie Mae. Both Fannie Mae and Freddie Mac are referred to as **government-sponsored enterprises (GSEs);** both are technically independent of the federal government, but both are subject to congressional oversight and, it turns out, to political pressure to do what Congress wants them to do.

The next key congressional action came in 1977 when the Community Reinvestment Act (CRA) was passed, a law that required banks to lend in all neighborhoods of the geographic areas where they operated, even where risks were likely to be much higher than the banks would normally undertake. In 1995, the CRA was amended so that banks were, in effect, compelled to ignore their lending standards when making loans in low-income and minority neighborhoods or else face the wrath of government regulators. Not long thereafter, Congress began putting considerable pressure on Fannie Mae and Freddie Mac to buy up the low-quality mortgages being made under the CRA in the hopes that this would encourage lenders to make still more high-risk loans. And indeed it did: The banks soon recognized that with the two GSEs standing ready to take the worst of their mortgages off their hands, they could earn hefty fees for originating the mortgages and then dump the risks of default off onto Fannie Mae and Freddie Mac. At this point, many potential lenders, including banks, savings and loans, and mortgage brokers, concluded that if Fannie Mae and Freddie Mac were happy to buy up risky mortgages at the drop of a hat, so to speak, then it was OK to hold on to some of the risky mortgages they were making. After all, these mortgages (called **subprime mortgages**) fattened **profits** with their above-average interest rates, and if the market turned sour, the GSEs would presumably stand ready to take them off lenders' hands.

STANDARDS? WHAT STANDARDS?

Thus it was regulatory and legislative pressure from the federal government (spearheaded by Congress) that pushed mortgage lenders to cut their lending standards in truly remarkable ways. For example, lenders historically insisted on down payments ranging from 5 to 20 percent on home loans. This gives borrowers an incentive to keep making monthly payments (lest they lose their down payment upon foreclosure), and it provides a cushion for the lender (to ensure that it gets all its money back upon foreclosure). Under pressure from federal regulators, however, lenders were induced to cut required down payments and even to make so-called piggyback loans, giving borrowers a second mortgage on top of the first to provide the cash for the down payment. In effect, down payments were driven to zero or close thereto.

But there was more. Federal regulators pushed banks to largely ignore mortgage applicants' credit histories if they were less than stellar, to forgo confirmation of applicants' current or past employment or income levels, to permit applicants to have lower income-to-loan ratios, and to count as part of income such sources as unemployment insurance and welfare payments, despite the temporary nature of such payments. Banks that had never before offered loans under such conditions soon made them routinely, pushed by the requirements of the CRA and pulled by the willingness of Fannie Mae and Freddie Mac to acquire the loans as soon as the ink was dry. And because the GSEs were so active in making the market for loans, many lenders felt comfortable making and holding on to such loans, even buying more loans from other lenders.

Congress's avowed intention in this process was to "help promote affordable housing," especially for low-income and minority individuals. Congress claimed to be particularly interested in making home ownership possible for people who had been renters all their lives. And indeed, a great many low-income and minority individuals were for the first time able to own their homes—at least for a while. But once the banks became comfortable making and disposing of high-risk loans, they quickly became amenable to making such loans to anyone who showed up, first-time buyer or not. And if the loan was to buy a house in a low-income or minority neighborhood, so much the better because of the possibility that it would keep the bean-counting regulators happy. Thus beginning in the late 1990s and accelerating rapidly in 2002 (when the house price trajectory turned up), speculators—people buying a second or third house in the hopes of selling quickly for a profit—became an increasingly important part of the market. Indeed, it is now estimated that one-quarter of all borrowers over this period were making speculative purchases of this sort.

Not surprisingly, speculators wanted to make low down payments and to obtain **adjustable-rate mortgages (ARMs).** Not only did ARMs offer slighter lower initial interest rates and payments (because borrowers absorbed the risk of higher rates in the future), but ARMs also gave lenders the flexibility to offer low "teaser" interest rates (and thus ultra-low payments) during the first few years of the mortgage. Such mortgages were considerably riskier for borrowers because of the prospect of higher payments later, when the mortgages "popped" (automatically adjusted their interest rates to full long-run levels). But by then, of course, speculators hoped to have sold for a profit and paid off the mortgage. The spread of ARMs, especially those with low teaser rates, was accelerated by people who bought homes hoping to refinance at a low fixed rate later, after rising home prices created equity for them in their houses.

MARKET COLLAPSE

All went well until 2005, when many of the early ARMs began to pop (with payments adjusting upward sharply). Some borrowers found they were unable to make the higher payments and were thus forced to sell their homes. This slowed the rise in house prices, making housing less attractive as an investment, which in turn reduced the speculative **demand** and put further downward pressure on prices. In markets such as Arizona, California, Florida, and Nevada, where speculative activity had been the greatest, house prices started to *fall,* and growing numbers of individuals (especially those with low or no down payments) found themselves "upside down," that is, owing more on their mortgages than their houses were worth. By the middle of 2006, the prudent financial course for such people was to stop making payments (especially on ARMs that had popped) and to simply walk away when the lender began foreclosure proceedings.

Many accounts of this process in the popular press have claimed that it is exclusively high-risk, subprime mortgages that were at the root of the crisis. This sounds sensible enough, because subprime mortgages have always had relatively high foreclosure rates; indeed, historically, the subprime foreclosure rate has been about eight times as high as the rate on prime mortgages (1.6 percent per year versus 0.2 percent per year). Hence subprime mortgages now, as in normal times, are disproportionately represented among foreclosures. But a closer look at the data also reveals that foreclosures on *both* types of mortgages shot upward in the middle of 2006, with foreclosures on subprime mortgages soon reaching 4 percent and those on prime mortgages hitting 0.5 percent. Thus it appears that both types of borrowers began to get in trouble at the same time; subprime mortgages were not uniquely affected.

A close look at the data also reveals another key fact: It is chiefly the borrowers who obtained adjustable-rate mortgages who caused the current mess. Prior to 2006, foreclosure rates on ARMs and on fixed-rate mortgages were very close to the same. But beginning in early 2006, even as the foreclosure rate on fixed-rate mortgages hardly budged, the rate on ARMs exploded: On prime ARMs, the rate leapt by a factor of five, while the foreclosure rate on subprime ARMs tripled. Moreover, it was the ARMs where foreclosures leapt initially first (at the very beginning of 2006). Thus it was forced sales on these homes that started the downward pressure on house prices, which gave more owners the incentive to walk away from their homes, which raised foreclosures, and so forth. Soon enough, the entire market had begun its meltdown.

By the time you read this, we expect (and hope!) that the housing market will have shown signs of recovery. But we also hope that the lesson of this episode will not be forgotten. The mortgage meltdown of 2006–2009 had its foundation laid by our very own Congress, which sought to subvert the housing market to achieve political goals. The methods used are perhaps little different than Congress usually employs when it desires to achieve politically popular social objectives. But the very real difference of this episode is the enormous social cost that it imposed on Americans of all races and all income levels. Millions of Americans had their hopes of home ownership first artificially raised and then cruelly dashed. The financial losses and emotional stresses inflicted on individuals, the blighted neighborhoods littered with abandoned houses, and the turmoil felt throughout the states most affected are all costs that will imprint the American scene for years to come.

FOR CRITICAL ANALYSIS

1. It seems likely that members of Congress, even the strongest supporters of the CRA and those who put the most pressure on the GSEs to buy high-risk mortgages, will likely escape being held responsible for any part of the mortgage meltdown. Can you suggest why?

2. In light of the fact that foreclosure rates have been much higher on ARMs than on fixed-rate mortgages, what do you predict will happen in the future to the proportion of mortgages that are of each type? Explain.

3. In effect, the CRA and the actions of Fannie Mae and Freddie Mac acted to subsidize home purchases by people who would otherwise not have purchased houses. All subsidies must be financed by taxes, implicit or explicit, on someone. Who is paying the "taxes" in this case? Explain.

CHAPTER 22

Deposit Insurance and Financial Markets

During the Panic of '08, the federal government announced a key new policy: It was insuring against loss all bank deposits up to $250,000 per account. So if your depository institution happened to be holding some toxic (possibly even worthless) **mortgage**-backed securities, you were home free. The bank could suffer terrible losses, even go out of business, and yet your accounts, up to $250,000 each, would be guaranteed by the full faith and of the United States government—which is to say, the U.S. taxpayer.

If you happened to notice the announcement of this policy, you may have wondered to yourself, why would the government do this? For example, although the federal government bought **shares of stock** in numerous banks at the same time, it most assuredly does not guarantee the value of those shares. Why treat deposits differently? A more subtle question is this: How do banks and other **depository institutions** behave differently because of this special deposit insurance? And you might even have wondered whether *your* behavior is likely to be any different because of this insurance. To get a handle on these and other questions, we must look back to the 1930s, before the notion of deposit insurance had even been conceived.

RUNS ON BANKS

Bank runs are defined as the simultaneous rush of depositors to convert their deposits into **currency.** Until the federal government set up deposit insurance in 1933, runs on banks were an infrequent but seemingly unavoidable occurrence, sometimes becoming widespread during economic **recessions.** The largest number of bank runs in modern history occurred during the Great Depression; as a result, more than *nine thousand* banks failed during the 1930s.

Just put yourself in the shoes of the depositor in a typical bank in 1930 and remember that you are a **creditor** of the bank. That is to say, your deposits in the bank are its **liabilities.** Suppose a rumor develops that the **assets** of the bank are not sufficient to cover its liabilities. In other words, the bank is, or will soon be, **insolvent.** Presumably, you are worried that you won't get your deposits back in the form of currency. Knowing this, you are likely to rush to the bank. All other depositors who hear about the bank's supposedly weak financial condition are likely to do the same thing.

This is the essence of a bank run: Regardless of the true state of the bank's financial condition, rumors or fears that a bank is in trouble can cause depositors to suddenly attempt to withdraw all of their funds. But many assets of a bank are in the form of loans that cannot immediately be converted into cash. Even if solvent, the bank is said to be **illiquid** because it doesn't have enough cash on hand to meet the demands of fearful depositors. And when it attempts to get that cash by selling some assets, any resulting decline in the market value of those assets can quickly turn a **solvent** bank into an insolvent one.

Bank runs can be disastrous for the economy because when they occur, the nation's **money supply** shrinks as people pull cash out of banks and stuff it under their mattresses (or wherever they think it might be safe). This is turn causes **aggregate demand** to fall, leading to higher unemployment, business failures, and yet more concerns for the solvency of banks. Quickly enough, the result can be an economic recession and widespread hardship.

DEPOSIT INSURANCE

When bank failures hit four thousand in 1933, the federal government decided to act to prevent further bank runs. That year, Congress passed, and the president signed into law, legislation creating the Federal Deposit Insurance Corporation (FDIC) and the next year created the Federal Savings and Loan Insurance Corporation (FSLIC). Many years later, in 1971, the National Credit Union Share Insurance Fund (NCUSIF) was created to insure credit union deposits, and in 1989, the FSLIC was replaced by the Savings Association Insurance Fund (SAIF). To make our discussion simple, we will focus only on the FDIC, but the general principles apply to all of these agencies.

When the FDIC was formed, it insured each account in a commercial bank against a loss of up to $2,500. That figure has been increased on seven different occasions, reaching $250,000 in 2008. The result of federal deposit insurance is that there has not been a widespread bank run in the United States since the Great Depression, despite numerous bank failures in the interim. Even during the Panic of 2008, when confidence in many financial institutions collapsed, federally insured depository institutions continued to operate; indeed, total deposits in them actually rose. The good news about federal deposit insurance is that it has prevented bank runs. But this has come at a significant cost, arising largely due to the unintended consequences of deposit insurance.

Adverse Selection

Suppose someone offers you what he or she claims is a great **investment** opportunity. That person tells you that if you invest $50,000, you will make a very high rate of return, say, 20 percent per year, much higher than the 3 percent your funds are currently earning elsewhere. No matter how much you trusted the person offering you this deal, you would probably do some serious investigation of the proposed investment before you handed over fifty thousand hard-earned dollars. You, like other people, would carefully evaluate the risk factors involved in this potential opportunity.

For example, if you use part of your **savings** to buy a house, you will undoubtedly have the structural aspects of the house checked out by an inspector before you sign on the dotted line. Similarly, if you planned to purchase an expensive piece of art, you surely would have an independent expert verify that the artwork is authentic. Typically, the same is true every time you place your accumulated savings into any potential investment: You look before you leap. In circumstances such as these, there is initially **asymmetric information**—in this case, the seller knows much more than the potential buyer. But with diligence, the buyer can eliminate much of this gap in knowledge and make a wise decision.

Now ask yourself, when is the last time you examined the financial condition or lending activities of the depository institution at which you have your checking or savings account? We predict that the answer is never. Indeed, why should you investigate? Because of federal deposit insurance, you know that even if the depository institution that has your funds is taking big risks, you are personally risking nothing. If that depository institution fails, the federal government will—with 100 percent certainty—make sure that you get 100 percent of your deposits back, up to the insurance limit.

So here we have it, the first unintended consequence of depository insurance. Depositors like you no longer have any substantial incentive to investigate the track record of the owners or managers of banks. You care little about whether they have a history of risky or imprudent behavior because at worst you may suffer some minor inconvenience if your bank fails. So unlike in the days before deposit insurance, the marketplace today does little to monitor or punish past performance of owners or managers of depository institutions. As a result, we tend to get **adverse selection**—instead of banks owned and operated by individuals who are prudent at making careful decisions on behalf of depositors, many of them end up run by people who have a high tolerance for taking big risks with other people's money.

Moral Hazard

Now let's look at bank managers' incentives to act cautiously when making loans. You must first note that the riskier the loan, the higher the interest rate that a bank can charge. For example, if a developing country with a blemished track record in paying its debts wishes to borrow from a U.S. depository institution, that country will have to pay a much higher interest rate than a less risky debtor. The same is true when a risky company comes looking for a loan: If it gets one at all, it will be at a higher-than-average interest rate.

When trying to decide which loan applicants should receive funds, bank managers must weigh the trade-off between risk and return. Poor credit risks offer high **profits** if they actually pay off their debts, but good credit risks are more likely to pay off their debts. The right choice means higher profits for the bank and likely higher salaries and promotions for the managers. The wrong choice means losses and perhaps insolvency for the bank and new, less desirable careers for the managers.

To understand how bank mangers' incentives are changed by deposit insurance—even for managers who otherwise would be prudent and conservative—consider two separate scenarios. In the first scenario, the bank manager is told to take $50,000 of depositors' funds to Las Vegas. The rules of the game are that she can bet however she wants, and the bank will *share* the winnings *and losses* equally with the deposit holders whose funds she has in trust. In the second scenario, the same bank manager with the same funds is given a different set of rules. In this case, the bank doesn't have to share in any of the losses, but it will share in any of the gains when betting in Las Vegas.

Under which set of rules do you think the bank officer will take the higher risks while betting in Las Vegas? Clearly, she will take higher risks in the second scenario, because her bank will not suffer at all if she loses the entire $50,000. Yet if she hits it big, say, by placing a successful bet on double-zero in roulette, her bank will share the profits, and she is likely to get a raise and a promotion.

Well, the second scenario is exactly the one facing the managers of federally insured depository institutions, especially since the fall of 2008. If they make risky loans, thereby earning, at least in the short run, higher profits, they share in the "winnings." The result for them is higher salaries. If, by contrast, some of these risky loans are not repaid, what is the likely outcome? The bank's losses are limited because the federal government (which is to say you, the taxpayer) will cover any shortfall between the bank's assets and its liabilities. Thus federal deposit insurance means that banks get to enjoy all of the profits of risk without bearing all of the consequences of that risk.

So the second unintended consequence of deposit insurance is to encourage **moral hazard.** Specifically, bank managers of all types (risk lovers or not) have an incentive to take higher risks in their lending policies than they otherwise would. Indeed, when the economy turned down in the early 1980s, we got to see the consequences of exactly this change in incentives. From 1985 until the beginning of 1993, 1,065 depository institutions failed, at an average rate of more than ten times that for the preceding forty years. The losses from these failures totaled billions of dollars—paid for in large part by you, the taxpayer.

What, then, might be expected from the 2008 insurance hike to $250,000? Well, in the short run, confidence in banks was renewed and depositors were encouraged to keep more funds in banks. This was good news, for it helped the economy adjust to the financial shocks of 2008–2009. But the bad news will be forthcoming in the long run: The higher deposit insurance limits will encourage both adverse selection (more risk-loving bank managers) and moral hazard (more risk-taking by bank managers of all stripes). Eventually, the lending standards of banks will deteriorate to the point that losses mount once again—paid for in part by you, the taxpayer.

PAYING FOR DEPOSIT INSURANCE

For the first sixty years or so of federal deposit insurance, all depository institutions were charged modest fees for their insurance coverage. Unfortunately, the fee that these depository institutions paid was completely unrelated to the riskiness of the loans they made. A bank that made loans to Microsoft was charged the same rate for deposit insurance as a bank that made loans to a startup company with no track record whatsoever. Hence not even the fees paid by banks for their insurance gave them any incentive to be prudent. This is completely unlike the case in private insurance markets, in which high-risk customers are charged higher premiums, giving them at least some incentive to become lower-risk customers.

In the early 1990s, the federal government made a feeble attempt to adjust fees for depository insurance to reflect the riskiness of their lending activities. But the political strength of the depository institutions prevented any fundamental change in the system. In 2008, the insurance fees paid by depository institutions were doubled, but even this was not enough to keep up with the added risks of the higher insurance limits. Just as important, more than 90 percent of all depository institutions pay the same insurance rate. Only the 9 percent who are the highest-risk pay a higher premium, and that amount is only 20 percent above the base rate—not nearly enough to cover the likely losses of those banks or enough to get them to change their risky behavior.

So while your banker is headed to Vegas, you'd better plan on staying at home to work. Sooner or later, as a U.S. taxpayer, your bill for deposit insurance will come due.

FOR CRITICAL ANALYSIS

1. If federal deposit insurance costs nothing, who pays when an insured depository institution fails and its depositors are nonetheless reimbursed for the full amount of their deposits?

2. In a world without deposit insurance, what are some of the mechanisms that would arise to "punish" bank managers who acted irresponsibly? (*Hint:* There are similar types of mechanisms for consumer goods and in the stock market.)

3. Explain how "experience rating" of insurance—charging higher premiums to higher-risk customers—affects the incidence of both adverse selection and moral hazard.

CHAPTER 23

How (Not) to Beat the Market

Within a few weeks in October 2008, the stock market lost more than 25 percent of its value. Virtually all commentators proclaimed it the most disastrous performance by the market since 1931, in the throes of the Great Depression. By the end of October, many observers were predicting that the market would surely decline by *another* 25 percent before any recovery could be expected. Yet within six weeks, the market had *risen* 15 percent. And in the months since, day-to-day and month-to-month movements in the stock market have been almost as volatile, sharing only one common feature: They have all been unpredictable.

Now, there is no doubt that a knowledge of macroeconomics can help you understand many important economic factors, including the determinants of the **unemployment rate** and the **inflation** rate and what causes changes in interest rates and the prices of the stocks issued by corporations. But sometimes people think that this level of understanding can take them a step further and enable them to *predict* the behavior of key macroeconomic variables in the future. It is true that when it comes to forecasting the unemployment rate, the inflation rate, or even the level of **real GDP,** the principles of macroeconomics can help. But when it comes to the stock market or interest rates, we want to emphatically (albeit sadly) inform you of this: Nothing you learn from this book (or any other) will enable you to "beat the market" by figuring out ahead of everyone else where stock prices, **bond** prices, or interest rates are going to be tomorrow or next year.

STOCKS, BONDS, AND BROKERS

Let's begin with the financial pages (sometimes called the business section) of the daily newspaper. There you will find column after column of information about the stocks and bonds of U.S. corporations. A **share of stock** in a corporation is simply a legal claim to a share of the corporation's future **profits;** owners of stocks are called **shareholders.** If there are 100,000 shares of stock in a company and you, as a shareholder, own 1,000 of them, then you own the right to 1 percent of that company's future profits.

A bond is a legal claim against a firm, entitling the bond owner to receive a fixed annual "coupon" payment, plus a lump-sum payment at the bond's maturity date. (Coupon payments on bonds get their name from the fact that bonds once had coupons attached to them when issued. Each year, the owner would clip a coupon off the bond and send it to the issuing firm in return for that year's interest payment.) Bonds are issued in return for funds lent to the firm. The coupon payments represent interest on the amount borrowed by the firm, and the lump-sum payment at maturity generally equals the amount originally borrowed. Bonds are *not* claims to the future profits of the firm; legally, the owners of the bonds, called **bondholders,** are to be paid whether the firm prospers or not. (To ensure this, bondholders generally must receive their coupon payments each year, plus any principal due, before *any* shareholders can receive their share of the firm's profits, called **dividends.**)

Now, suppose that in your quest for riches, you decide to buy some shares of stock in a corporation. How should you choose which corporation's stock to buy? One way is to consult a specialist in stocks, called a **stockbroker.** Such brokers have access to an enormous amount of information. They can tell you what lines of business specific corporations are in, who the firms' major competitors are, how profitable the firms have been in the past, and whether their stocks' prices have risen or fallen. If pressed, they will probably be willing to recommend which stocks to buy. Throughout your discussion, the broker's opinion will sound highly informed and authoritative.

Strange as it may seem, though, a broker's investment advice is not likely to be any better than anyone else's. In fact, *the chances of the broker's being right are no greater than the chances of your being right!* Indeed, you are just as likely to get rich (or avoid going broke) by throwing darts at the financial pages of your newspaper. Let's see why.

THE MAGIC OF THE DARTS

Some years ago, the editors of *Forbes,* a respected business magazine, taped the financial pages of a major newspaper to a wall and threw darts at the portion listing stock prices. They hit the stocks of twenty-eight different companies and invested a hypothetical $1,000 in each. When the editors halted their experiment, the original $28,000 had grown to $132,000—a gain of 370 percent. Over the same period, the Dow Jones Industrial Average (a leading measure of the stock market's overall performance) grew less than 40 percent in value. Perhaps even more impressive, *Forbes*'s random selection of stocks outperformed the recommended stock portfolios of most of the stock market–forecasting "gurus."

More recently, the editors of the *Wall Street Journal,* a major financial newspaper, tried a similar experiment. Each month, they invited four stockbrokers to recommend a stock to buy; the four stocks became the "experts' portfolio" for the month. Then the editors threw four darts at the financial pages of their newspaper to select four stocks that became the "darts' portfolio" for the month. Over time, the particular expert brokers changed, depending on how well their picks performed relative to the darts' portfolio. Any broker whose stock beat the darts got to pick again the next month. Any expert beaten by the darts was replaced the next month by a new broker. At six-month intervals, the newspaper tallied up the performances of the experts versus the darts. After several years of running the experiment, the general result was this: Although the experts beat the darts over the long haul, the winning margin was tiny. Moreover, there were several six-month periods in which the darts actually *outperformed* the experts. How did the darts do it?

Buy Low, Sell High

Suppose that you, and you alone, noticed that the price of a particular stock moved in a predictable manner. Specifically, assume that the price *rose* 5 percent on even-numbered days and *fell* 5 percent on odd-numbered days, resulting in (approximately) no average change over time. Knowing this fact, how do you make money? You simply buy shares of the stock just before their price is due to rise and sell those shares just before it is due to fall. If you start the year with $1,000 and reinvest your profits, following this strategy would yield profits in excess of $500,000 by the end of the year. If you successfully continue this strategy for a second year, your **wealth** would exceed $250 million!

Of course, as your wealth accumulates—"buying low and selling high"—your purchases and sales would start to affect the price of the stock. Your purchases would drive up the low prices, and your sales would drive down the high prices. Ultimately, your buying and selling in response to predictable patterns would *eliminate* those patterns, and there would be no profit potential left to exploit. This is *exactly* what happens in the stock market—except it happens far faster than a single person could accomplish alone.

A Random Walk down Wall Street

At any point in time, there are tens of thousands, perhaps millions, of people looking for any bit of information that will help them forecast the future prices of stocks. Responding to any information that seems useful, these people try to "buy low and sell high," just as you would like to do. As a result, all publicly available information that might be used to forecast stock prices gets taken into account, leaving no predictable profits. Furthermore, because there are so many people involved in this process, it occurs quite swiftly. Indeed, there is evidence that all information entering the market is fully incorporated into stock prices within *less than a minute* of its arrival.

The result is that stock prices tend to follow a **random walk**—which is to say that the best forecast of tomorrow's price is today's price plus a random component. Although large values of the random component are less likely than small values, nothing else about its magnitude or sign (positive or negative) can be predicted. Indeed, the random component of stock prices exhibits behavior much like what would occur if you rolled a pair of dice and subtracted 7 from the resulting score. *On average,* the dice will total 7, so after you subtract 7, the average result will be zero. It is true that rolling a 12 or a 2 (yielding a net score of + 5 or –5) is less likely than rolling an 8 or a 6 (producing a net score of +1 or –1). Nevertheless, positive and negative net scores are equally likely, and the expected net score is zero.[1]

It is worth emphasizing that the bond market operates every bit as efficiently as the stock market. That is, investors in bonds study the available information and use whatever might help them forecast future bond prices. Because they exploit this information up to the point that the added benefits of doing so are just matched by the added costs, there remains no publicly available information that can be used profitably to improve bond price forecasts. As a result, bond prices, like stock prices, follow a random walk. Moreover, because interest rates are inextricably linked to the prices of bonds, interest rates also follow a random walk.

What Are Those People Doing?

In light of this discussion, two questions arise. First, are all the efforts put into forecasting stock and bond prices simply a waste? The answer is no. From a social viewpoint, this effort is productive because it helps ensure

---

1. Strictly speaking, stock prices follow a random walk with **drift;** that is, on average, they rise at a real (inflation-adjusted) rate of about 3 percent per year over long periods of time. This drift, which is the average compensation investors receive for deferring **consumption,** can be thought of as the 7 that comes up on average when two dice are rolled.

that **asset** prices correctly reflect all available information and thus that **resources** are allocated efficiently. From a private standpoint, the effort is also rewarding, just as any other productive activity is rewarding. At the margin, the added gains from trying to forecast future stock and bond prices are exactly equal to the added costs; there are no unexploited profit opportunities. Unless you happen to have some unique ability that makes you better than others, you will earn only enough to cover your costs— but, of course, the same is true of growing wheat or selling women's shoes. So absent some special ability, you are just as well-off investing in the market based on the roll of the dice or the throw of a dart.

The second question is a bit trickier: Isn't there any way to "beat the market"? The answer is yes—but only if you have **inside information,** knowledge that is unavailable to the public. Suppose, for example, that your best friend is in charge of new product development for Mousetrap, Inc., a firm that just last night invented a mousetrap superior to all others on the market. No one but your friend—and now you—are aware of this. You could indeed make a killing with this information by purchasing shares of Mousetrap, Inc., and then selling them (at a higher price) as soon as the invention is publicly announced. There is one problem: Stock trading based on such inside information is illegal, punishable by substantial fines and even imprisonment. Unless you happen to have a stronger-than-average desire for a long vacation in a federal prison, our money-making advice to you is simple: Invest in the mousetrap after it hits the market—and throw darts in the meantime.

FOR CRITICAL ANALYSIS

1. Why do you think the government prohibits insider trading?

2. When the prices of stocks fall, newspapers often report that the decline in prices was caused by a "wave of selling." By the definition of exchange, every sale must be accompanied by a purchase. Why, then, do the newspapers not report that the decline in stock prices was caused by a "wave of purchasing"?

3. If stockbrokers cannot "beat the market," why do people use their services?

CHAPTER 24

Credit-Card Crunch

By the time you read this, you may already have had a credit-card application denied or an existing card canceled. No, we are not talking about the credit-card cutbacks that resulted from the recession of 2007–2009. We are referring to the effects of new **Federal Reserve** regulations (expanded by Congress) that are said to benefit you but have in many cases had exactly the opposite effect.

We speak of federal restrictions on the interest rates and fees that credit-card firms may charge their customers. Effective in 2010, such companies are sharply limited in their ability to raise interest rates on existing credit balances, even if interest rates soar elsewhere in the economy. Moreover, the companies are limited in the fees they may charge customers who have little or no credit background or customers who have a troubled credit history. The result is a reduction in the credit available and credit that is more, not less, expensive to obtain.

CREDIT-CARD COMPLAINTS

If you have had a credit card for several years or know people who have, you have likely heard one or more "horror stories" about outrageous late fees or sky-high interest rates or other charges imposed by credit-card companies. Some of these incidents are no doubt the result of unscrupulous practices by companies that prey on naïve consumers. Some companies have actually been able to commit fraud under the guise of being a credit-card issuer.

But the vast majority of all credit cards are issued by companies that are in the business for the long haul. The interest rates and fees they charge are competitively determined and dependent on the (often substantial) risks of dealing with their cardholders. The practices of companies such as these are generally beyond reproach. Nevertheless, in 2008, the Fed and the other federal agencies that regulate credit-card firms decided that the fly-by-night operators needed to be reined in. Congress got involved in 2009, passing legislation that buttressed the Fed's rules. Hence a sweeping new series of regulations have been instituted, taking full effect in 2010. A positive result of the regulations is that some customers will be protected from fraudulent activities; those elements of the new rules have proved beneficial to a limited set of consumers. But the new rules also severely hamper the way the *reputable* companies do business. The result of this has been less credit and more expensive credit—a lesson you may already have learned the hard way.

Price Controls on Credit Cards

Among the myriad details of the new credit-card regulations, the key provisions are those that limit the interest rates and fees that companies can charge. For example, firms are limited in the circumstances under which they can raise the interest rates they charge. Moreover, higher rates can only be applied to new charges, not to past balances—even if market interest rates in general have increased or the borrower has become a worse credit risk since the card was issued. Credit-card firms are also limited in the fees they may charge when customers exceed their preset credit limits and the fees that they may charge for the subprime credit cards they issue to people with bad credit ratings.

As a practical matter, these provisions effectively act as **price controls**—legal limits on the prices that may be charged for goods or services. Here the controls are upper limits on prices, which means that interest rates and fees on credit cards are kept below their competitive levels. This causes firms' revenues to fall relative to their costs, which in turn reduces **profits** and discourages the firms from supplying the good in question, in this case consumer credit. On the other side of the market, because the legal maximum price is below the equilibrium price, people respond according to the law of **demand:** They try to obtain more of the good. In this case, consumers try to borrow more via credit cards. Because the quantity demanded rises and the quantity supplied falls, an excess quantity demanded is the result: People want to acquire far more than firms are willing to provide. In this case, desired borrowing goes up while desired lending goes down. Ultimately, the excess quantity demanded must be rationed somehow. The result is a series of readily predicted—and generally wasteful—consequences in the market. Let's see what those are.

Less Credit

The first and foremost effect of the price controls is to reduce the amount of credit available to consumers. Firms have reduced the number of credit-card offers they make, for example, because the expected profit from those cards is reduced by the limits on interest rates and fees. Many thousands of customers have had existing cards canceled because the new regulations made those cards unprofitable for the issuing companies. Credit-card companies are also denying more consumer applications for credit cards because the firms are no longer able to cover the expected costs of issuing and servicing the cards of high-risk customers. And finally, when the companies do issue credit cards, they are generally imposing lower credit limits (maximum balances that consumers may have). This is because, for a customer with any given credit rating, the higher the credit balances, the higher the expected costs for the supplier of credit. Quite simply, as credit balances rise relative to a person's ability to pay, the chances rise that there will be late payments or no payments at all. Under the new rules, firms are less able to recoup those higher losses, so they have cut credit limits.

More Expensive Credit

Paradoxically, the net effect of limits on interest rates and fees has been to *raise* effective costs for many, perhaps most, customers. This is because the limits on interest rates and fees have reduced the amount of credit supplied and thus produced an excess quantity demanded, which, as we have noted, must be rationed somehow. To achieve this rationing, the cost to consumers of that credit must rise. There is simply no way to avoid this in a world of **scarcity.**

Some of these higher costs have come in the form of more onerous application procedures, which now require more documentation and verification. But there is another and even more important way that the cost of credit is driven up by the price controls on credit cards. Many people have been forced to turn to consumer finance companies, which typically charge interest rates of 30 to 40 percent per year, rather than the 15 to 30 percent routinely charged on credit-card balances. In other instances, the new regulations have made life even worse than this for people with bad credit histories. Many of these individuals are now forced to obtain so-called payday loans.[1] These loans, usually made for one week to one

---

1. One variant of these loans is sometimes called a "check into cash" transaction. Here is a simple example: The borrower receives $100 in cash today in return for writing the lender a personal check for $120, which the lender agrees not to cash until two weeks have passed. This deal translates into an implicit interest rate of about 10 percent *per week.*

month at a time, often carry interest rates as high as 500 percent per year! Thus some of the people supposedly helped by the new regulations actually end up paying far more for their credit than they did before—as much as twenty times more.

THE POOR GET POORER

Of course, the developments of which we have spoken so far—reduced credit opportunities and higher credit costs—are not borne equally by all potential customers. In particular, affluent customers with top credit ratings have been essentially untouched. The fees and interest charges most affected by the new regulations are those that apply to people with poor credit ratings—generally, low-income individuals. As a result, it is these people, the ones supposedly helped, who are actually hurt the most. It is their applications that are being denied, and they are the ones turning to consumer finance companies and payday loan operations. For the well-to-do, it is business as usual. For the disadvantaged, it is one more example of a government regulation for which the principal consequences are "unintended," which is to say, directly contrary to the avowed purpose of the regulations.

WASTED RESOURCES

Not surprisingly, the new limits on interest rates and fees must be enforced, so the regulations have spurred growth in the bureaucracies of the Fed, the Office of Thrift Supervision, and the Federal Deposit Insurance Corporation. The credit-card firms also face higher costs due to these regulations because they must demonstrate compliance with them and keep additional records. And because caps on rates and fees have forced the firms to conduct more credit checks and require more documentation, additional resources are being expended here. These are all resources that could have been put to good use elsewhere but are instead being used to implement and enforce the new price controls.

SAVERS LOSE TOO

Clearly, the new rules on interest rates and fees reduce the amount of credit extended to consumers. This means that the people who ultimately provide the funds for that credit lose too, because there is less demand for their savings. You might think that it is the credit-card companies that are the ultimate source of those funds, but you would be wrong. In fact, it is ordinary savers who provide the funds that are lent to consumers by means of credit cards. The credit-card companies merely act as intermediaries, moving the funds from savers to borrowers. Thus people who have savings accounts or money market funds or small certificates of deposit are all now earning lower interest rates on their deposits because the interest rates paid by borrowers are controlled by the government.

THE BOTTOM LINE

The new price controls for credit cards have made the market less effective in allocating funds from savers to borrowers. As a result, our **wealth** as a society has been reduced. But at least the new rules enable us to see some key public policy principles in action.

There is no free lunch. It is nice to think that with the stroke of the regulatory pen, we might "make it so." But in a world of scarcity, that simply doesn't happen. Price controls distort incentives, raise costs, and reduce opportunities. Moreover, they are costly to implement and enforce, and they generally do not accomplish their avowed purpose, which is to help the disadvantaged.

People respond to incentives. When there is a reduction in the profits of making loans via credit cards, fewer of those loans are made. And when that happens, people have an incentive to turn elsewhere for funds. Even though those alternative sources are far more costly, they are not as costly for the borrowers as the option of doing without. And so people do what they must because they can no longer do what they wish.

Things aren't always what they seem. A superficial look at the credit market seems to suggest that people are better off because many of the people who do still have credit cards are paying lower interest and lower fees. But such a look misses the higher costs people are paying elsewhere and the losses that result because some people are unable to obtain any credit at all due to the new controls.

Policies always have unintended consequences, and so their net benefits are almost always lower than anticipated. Surely Congress and policymakers at the Fed didn't go into the regulatory process intending to reduce credit opportunities for low-income individuals. Nor did they hope to increase the credit costs that such individuals must actually bear to obtain credit under the new rules. But this is exactly what has happened, meaning that the rules produced fewer net benefits than the authors of the new rules intended.

So if you are one of the people who was turned down for a credit card or had one canceled or was forced to turn to a higher-cost source of credit, there should be one consolation in all this: At least you have received an education in how the public policy process works in practice.

FOR CRITICAL ANALYSIS

1. Why do you suppose the government regulates interest rates on consumer credit (as with credit cards) but generally does not do so with commercial credit (as with loans to businesses)?

2. What do controls on interest rates do to the incentive of consumers to lie on their credit applications in an effort to qualify for a credit card?

3. More than sixty-five thousand individuals and businesses submitted comments on the Fed's regulations when they were first proposed. How might a look at these comments (which are a matter of public record) help you identify individuals and businesses who are likely to gain or lose as a result of the regulations?

4. Why would a limit on interest rates on *old* credit-card balances reduce the incentive of firms to issue *new* cards?

PART FIVE

Globalization and International Finance

CHAPTER 25

The Opposition to Globalization

The period since the early 1990s has been a time of great change on the international trade front. The North American Free Trade Agreement (NAFTA), for example, substantially reduced **trade barriers** among citizens of Canada, the United States, and Mexico. On a global scale, the Uruguay Round of the General Agreement on Tariffs and Trade (GATT) was ratified by 117 nations including the United States. Under the terms of this agreement, the **World Trade Organization (WTO),** whose membership now numbers more than 150, replaced GATT, and **tariffs** were cut worldwide. Agricultural **subsidies** were also reduced, and patent protections were extended. The WTO has also established arbitration boards to settle international disputes over trade issues.

THE GAINS FROM TRADE

Many economists believe that both NAFTA and the agreements reached during the Uruguay Round were victories not only for free trade and **globalization** (the integration of national economies into an international economy) but also for the citizens of the participating nations. Nevertheless, many noneconomists, particularly politicians, opposed these agreements, so it is important to understand what is beneficial about NAFTA, the Uruguay Round, the WTO, and free trade and globalization.

Voluntary trade creates new **wealth.** In voluntary trade, both parties in an exchange gain. They give up something of lesser value to them in return for something of greater value to them. In this sense, exchanges are always unequal. But it is this unequal nature of exchange that is the source of the increased **productivity** and higher wealth that occur whenever trade takes place. When we engage in exchange, what we give up is worth less than what we get—if this were not true, we would not have traded. What is true for us is also true for our trading partner, meaning that the partner is better off, too. (Of course, sometimes after an exchange, you may believe that you were mistaken about the value of what you just received—this is called *buyer's remorse,* but it does not affect our discussion.)

Free trade encourages individuals to employ their talents and abilities in the most productive manner possible and to exchange the fruits of their efforts. The **gains from trade** arise from one of the fundamental ideas in economics: A nation gains from doing what it can do best *relative to other nations,* that is, by specializing in those endeavors in which it has a **comparative advantage.** Trade encourages individuals and nations to discover ways to specialize so that they can become more productive and enjoy higher incomes. Increased productivity and the subsequent increase in the rate of **economic growth** are exactly what the signatories of the Uruguay Round and NAFTA sought—and are obtaining—by reducing trade barriers and thus increasing globalization.

KEEPING THE COMPETITION OUT

Despite the enormous gains from exchange, some people (sometimes a great many of them) routinely oppose free trade, particularly in the case of international trade. This opposition comes in many guises, but they all basically come down to one: When our borders are open to trade with other nations, this exposes some individuals and businesses in our nation to more **competition.** Most firms and workers hate competition, and who can blame them? After all, if a firm can keep competitors out, its **profits** are sure to stay the same or even rise. Also, if workers can prevent competition from other sources, they can enjoy higher wages and perhaps a larger selection of jobs. So the real source of most opposition to globalization is that the opponents of trade dislike the competition that comes with it. This position is not immoral or unethical, but it is not altruistic or noble, either. It is based on self-interest, pure and simple.

Opposition to globalization is nothing new, by the way. In the twentieth century, it culminated most famously in the Smoot-Hawley Tariff Act of 1930. This federal statute was a classic example of **protectionism**—an effort to protect a subset of U.S. producers at the expense of consumers and other producers. It included tariff schedules for over twenty thousand products, raising taxes on affected imports by an average of 52 percent.

The Smoot-Hawley Tariff Act encouraged so-called *beggar-thy-neighbor* policies by the rest of the world. Such policies are an attempt to improve (a portion of) one's domestic economy at the expense of foreign countries' economies. In this case, tariffs were imposed to discourage imports in the hope that domestic import-competing industries would benefit. France, the Netherlands, Switzerland and the United Kingdom, soon adopted beggar-thy-neighbor policies to counter the American ones. The result was a massive reduction in international trade. According to many economists, this caused a worldwide worsening of the Great Depression.

Opponents of globalization sometimes claim that beggar-thy-neighbor policies really do benefit the United States by protecting import-competing industries. In general, this claim is not correct. It is true that *some* Americans benefit from such policies, but two large groups of Americans lose. First, the purchasers of imports and import-competing goods suffer from the higher prices and reduced selection of goods and suppliers caused by tariffs and import **quotas.** Second, the decline in imports caused by protectionism also causes a decline in *exports,* thereby harming firms and workers in these industries. This result follows directly from one of the fundamental propositions in international trade: *In the long run, imports are paid for by exports.* This proposition simply states that when one country buys goods and services from the rest of the world (imports), the rest of the world eventually wants goods from that country (exports) in exchange. Given this fundamental proposition, a corollary becomes obvious: *Any restriction on imports leads to a reduction in exports.* Thus any extra business for import-competing industries gained as a result of tariffs or quotas means at least as much business *lost* for exporting industries.

THE ARGUMENTS AGAINST GLOBALIZATION

Opponents of globalization often raise a variety of objections in their efforts to reduce it. For example, it is sometimes claimed that foreign companies engage in **dumping,** which is selling their goods in the United States "below cost." The first question to ask when such charges are made is, below *whose* cost? Clearly, if the foreign firm is selling in the United States, it must be offering the good for sale at a price that is at or below the costs of U.S. firms; otherwise it could not induce Americans to buy it. But the ability of individuals or firms to obtain goods at lower cost is one of the *benefits* of free trade, not one of its harmful aspects.

What about claims that import sales are taking place at prices below the foreign company's costs? This amounts to arguing that the owners of the foreign company are voluntarily giving some of their wealth to us, namely, the difference between their costs and the (lower) price they charge us. It is possible, though unlikely, that they might wish to do this, perhaps because this could be the cheapest way of getting us to try a product that we would not otherwise purchase. But even supposing it is true, why would we want to refuse this gift? As a nation, we are richer if we accept it. Moreover, it is a gift that will be offered for only a short time: There is no point in selling at prices below cost unless the seller hopes to soon raise the price profitably above cost!

Another argument sometimes raised against globalization is that the goods are produced abroad using "unfair" labor practices (such as the use of child labor) or production processes that do not meet U.S. environmental standards. Such charges are sometimes true. But we must remember two things here. First, although we may find the use of child labor (or perhaps sixty-hour workweeks with no overtime pay) objectionable, such practices were at one time commonplace in the United States. They were common here for the same reason they are currently practiced abroad: The people involved were (or are) too poor to do otherwise. Some families in developing nations cannot survive unless all family members contribute. As unfortunate as this situation is, if we insist on imposing our values and attitudes—shaped in part by our extraordinarily high wealth—on peoples whose wealth is far lower than ours, we run the risk of making them worse off even as we think we are helping them.

Similar considerations apply to environmental standards. Individuals' and nations' willingness to pay for environmental quality is very much shaped by their wealth. Environmental quality is a **normal good;** this means that people who are rich (such as Americans) want to consume more of it per capita than people who are poor. Insisting that other nations meet environmental standards that we find acceptable is much like insisting that they wear the clothes we wear, use the modes of transportation we prefer, and consume the foods we like. The few people who can afford it will indeed be living in the style to which we are accustomed, but most people in developing countries will not be able to afford anything like that style.

There is one important exception to this argument. When foreign air or water pollution is generated near enough to our borders (for example, in Mexico or Canada) to cause harm to Americans, good public policy presumably dictates that we seek to treat that pollution as though it were being generated inside our borders.

Our point is not that foreign labor or environmental standards are, or should be, irrelevant to Americans. Instead, our point is that achieving high standards of either is costly, and trade restrictions are unlikely to be the most efficient or effective way to achieve them. Just as important, labor standards and environmental standards are all too often raised as smokescreens to hide the real motive: keeping the competition out.

WHY ARE ANTITRADE MEASURES PASSED?

If globalization is beneficial and restrictions on trade are generally harmful, how does legislation such as the Smoot-Hawley Tariff Act and other restrictions on international trade ever get passed? The explanation is that because foreign competition often affects a narrow and specific import-competing industry, such as textiles, shoes, or automobiles, trade restrictions are crafted to benefit a narrow, well-defined group of economic agents. For example, limits on imports of Japanese automobiles in the 1980s chiefly benefited the Big Three automakers in this country: General Motors, Ford, and Chrysler. Similarly, long-standing quotas that limit imports of sugar benefit a handful of large U.S. sugar producers. Because of the concentrated benefits that accrue when Congress votes in favor of trade restrictions, sufficient funds can be raised in those industries to aggressively lobby members of Congress to impose those restrictions.

The eventual reduction in exports that must follow is normally spread throughout all export industries. Consequently, no specific group of workers, managers, or shareholders in export industries will be motivated to contribute funds to lobby Congress to reduce international trade restrictions. Furthermore, although consumers of imports and import-competing goods lose due to trade restrictions, they, too, are typically a diffuse group of individuals, none of whom will be greatly affected individually by any particular import restriction. This simultaneous existence of concentrated benefits and diffuse costs led Mark Twain to observe long ago that the free traders win the arguments but the **protectionists** win the votes.

Of course, the protectionists don't win *all* the votes—after all, about one-seventh of the U.S. economy is based on international trade. Despite the opposition to free trade that comes from many quarters, its benefits to the economy as a whole are so great that it is unthinkable that we might do away with international trade altogether. Both economic theory and empirical evidence clearly indicate that on balance, Americans will be better off with freer trade achieved through such developments as NAFTA and the WTO.

FOR CRITICAL ANALYSIS

1. For a number of years, Japanese automakers voluntarily limited the number of cars they exported to the United States. What effect do you think this had on Japanese imports of U.S. cars and U.S. exports of goods and services *other than* automobiles?

2. Until a few years ago, U.S. cars exported to Japan had the driver controls on the left side (as in the United States). The Japanese, however, drive on the left side of the road, so Japanese cars sold in Japan have the driver controls on the right side. Suppose the Japanese tried to sell their cars in the United States with the driver controls on the right side. What impact would this likely have on their sales in this country? Do you think the unwillingness of U.S. carmakers to put the driver controls on the "correct" side for exports to Japan had any effect on their sales of cars in that country?

3. Keeping in mind the key propositions of globalization outlined in this chapter, what is the likely impact of international trade restrictions on the following variables in the United States: employment, the **unemployment rate, real GDP,** and the **price level?** Explain your responses.

CHAPTER 26

The $750,000 Job

In even-numbered years, particularly years evenly divisible by 4, politicians of all persuasions are apt to give long-winded speeches about the need to protect U.S. jobs from the evils of **globalization**. To accomplish this goal, we are encouraged to "buy American." If further encouragement is needed, we are told that if we do not voluntarily reduce the amount of imported goods we purchase, the government will impose (or make more onerous) **tariffs** (taxes) on imported goods or **quotas** (quantity restrictions) that physically limit imports. The objective of this exercise is to "save U.S. jobs."

Unlike African elephants or blue whales, U.S. jobs are in no danger of becoming extinct. There are virtually an unlimited number of potential jobs in the U.S. economy, and there always will be. Some of these jobs are not very pleasant, and many others do not pay very well, but there will always be employment of some sort as long as there is **scarcity**. So when a steelworker making $72,000 per year says that imports of foreign steel should be reduced to save his job, what he really means is this: He wants to be protected from **competition** so that he can continue his present employment at the same or a higher salary rather than move to a different job that has less desirable working conditions or pays less. There is nothing wrong with the steelworker's goal (better working conditions and higher pay), but it has nothing to do with "saving jobs."

THE GAINS FROM GLOBALIZATION

In any discussion of the consequences of international trade restrictions, it is essential to remember two facts. First, *we pay for imports with exports*. It is true that in the short run, we can sell off **assets** or borrow from abroad if we happen to import more goods and services than we export. But we have only a finite amount of assets to sell, and foreigners will not wait forever for us to pay our bills. Ultimately, our accounts can be settled only if we *provide* (export) goods and services to the trading partners from whom we *purchase* (import) goods and services. Trade, after all, involves a *quid pro quo* (literally, "something for something").

The second point to remember is that *voluntary trade is mutually beneficial to the trading partners.* If we restrict international trade, we reduce those benefits, both for our trading partners and for ourselves. One way these reduced benefits are manifested is in the form of curtailed employment opportunities for workers. The reasoning is simple. Other countries will buy our goods only if they can market theirs because they, too, have to export goods to pay for their imports. Thus any U.S. restrictions on imports to this country—via tariffs, quotas, or other means—ultimately cause a reduction in our exports because other countries will be unable to pay for our goods. This implies that import restrictions must inevitably decrease the size of our export sector. So imposing trade restrictions to save jobs in import-competing industries has the effect of costing jobs in export industries. Most studies have shown that the net effect seems to be reduced employment overall.

THE ADVERSE EFFECTS OF TRADE RESTRICTIONS

Just as important, import restrictions impose costs on U.S. consumers as a whole. By reducing competition from abroad, quotas, tariffs, and other trade restraints push up the prices of foreign goods and enable U.S. producers to hike their own prices. Perhaps the best-documented example of this effect is found in the automobile industry, where "voluntary" restrictions on Japanese imports were in place for more than a decade.

Due in part to the enhanced quality of imported cars, sales of domestically produced automobiles fell from 9 million units in 1978 to an average of 6 million units per year between 1980 and 1982. Profits of U.S. automakers plummeted as well, and some incurred substantial losses. The automobile manufacturers' and autoworkers' unions demanded protection from import competition. Politicians from automobile-producing states rallied to their cause. The result was a "voluntary" agreement by Japanese car companies (the most important competitors of U.S. firms) to restrict their U.S. sales to 1.68 million units per year. This agreement—which amounted to a quota, even though it never officially bore that name—began in April 1981 and continued into the 1990s in various forms.

Robert W. Crandall, an economist with the Brookings Institution, estimated how much this voluntary trade restriction cost U.S. consumers in higher car prices. According to his estimates, the reduced supply of Japanese cars pushed their prices up by $1,500 per car, measured in 1996 dollars. The higher prices of Japanese imports in turn enabled domestic producers to hike their prices an average of $600 per car. The total tab in the first full year of the program was $6.5 billion. Crandall also estimated that about twenty-six thousand jobs in automobile-related industries were saved by the voluntary import restrictions. Dividing $6.5 billion by twenty-six thousand jobs yields a cost to consumers of more than $250,000 *per year* for every job saved in the automobile industry. U.S. consumers could have saved nearly $2 billion on their car purchases each year if instead of implicitly agreeing to import restrictions, they had simply given $75,000 to every autoworker whose job was preserved by the voluntary import restraints.

The same types of calculations have been made for other industries. Tariffs in the apparel industry were increased between 1977 and 1981, saving the jobs of about 116,000 U.S. apparel workers at a cost of $45,000 per job each year. The cost of **protectionism** has been even higher in other industries. Jobs preserved in the glassware industry due to trade restrictions cost $200,000 apiece each year. In the maritime industry, the yearly cost of trade restriction is $290,000 per job. In the steel industry, the cost of preserving a job has been estimated at an astounding $750,000 per year. If free trade were permitted, each worker losing a job could be given a cash payment of half that amount each year, and consumers would still save a lot of **wealth.**

THE REAL IMPACT ON JOBS

What is more, none of these cost studies has attempted to estimate the ultimate impact of import restrictions on the flow of exports, the number of jobs lost in the export sector, and thus the total number of jobs gained or lost.

Remember that imports pay for exports and that our imports are the exports of our trading partners. So when imports to the United States are restricted, our trading partners will necessarily buy less of what we produce. The resulting decline in export sales means fewer jobs in exporting industries. And the total reduction in trade leads to fewer jobs for workers such as stevedores (who unload ships) and truck drivers (who carry goods to and from ports). On both counts—the overall cut in trade and the accompanying decline in exports—protectionism leads to job losses that might not be obvious immediately.

In 1983, Congress tried to pass a "domestic-content" bill for automobiles. The legislation would have required that cars sold in the

United States have a minimum percentage of their components manufactured and assembled in this country. Proponents of the legislation argued that it would have protected 300,000 jobs in the U.S. automobile manufacturing and auto parts supply industries. Yet the legislation's supporters failed to recognize the negative impact of the bill on trade in general and its ultimate impact on U.S. export industries. A U.S. Department of Labor study did recognize these impacts, estimating that the domestic-content legislation would have cost more jobs in trade-related and export industries than it protected in import-competing businesses. Congress ultimately decided not to impose a domestic-content requirement for cars sold in the United States.

THE LONG-RUN FAILURE OF IMPORT CONTROLS

In principle, trade restrictions are imposed to provide economic help to specific industries and to increase employment in those industries. Ironically, the long-term effects may be just the opposite. Researchers at the **World Trade Organization (WTO)** examined employment in three industries that have been heavily protected throughout the world: textiles, clothing, and iron and steel. Despite stringent **protectionist** measures, employment in these industries actually declined during the period of protection, in some cases dramatically. In textiles, employment fell 22 percent in the United States and 46 percent in the European Common Market (the predecessor of the **European Union**). Employment losses in the clothing industry ranged from 18 percent in the United States to 56 percent in Sweden. Losses in the iron and steel industry ranged from 10 percent in Canada to 54 percent in the United States. In short, the WTO researchers found that restrictions on free trade were no guarantee against job losses, even in the industries supposedly being protected.

The evidence seems clear: The cost of protecting jobs in the short run is enormous, and in the long run, it appears that jobs cannot be protected, especially if one considers all aspects of protectionism. Free trade is a tough platform on which to run for office, but it is likely to be the one that will yield the most general benefits if implemented. Of course, this does not mean that politicians will embrace it. So we end up "saving jobs" at an annual cost of $750,000 each.

FOR CRITICAL ANALYSIS

1. If it would be cheaper to give each steelworker $375,000 per year in cash than impose restrictions on steel imports, why do we have the import restrictions rather than the cash payments?

2. Most U.S. imports and exports travel through our seaports at some point. How do you predict that members of Congress from coastal states would vote on proposals to restrict international trade? What other information would you want to know in making such a prediction?

3. Who gains and who loses from import restrictions? In answering, you should consider both consumers and producers in both the country that imposes the restrictions and in the other countries affected by them. Also, be sure to take into account the effects of import restrictions on *export* industries.

CHAPTER 27

The Trade Deficit

The idea is not new; indeed, it goes back centuries: Selling to foreigners is better than buying from them. That is, exports are good and imports are bad. Today, reading between the lines of the press coverage about international trade reveals that political and public thinking is not much different than it was three hundred years ago. The **mercantilists** who ruled public policy from the sixteenth through eighteenth centuries felt that the only proper objective of international trade was to expand exports without expanding imports. Their goal was to acquire large amounts of the gold that served as the money of their era. The mercantilists felt that a **trade surplus** (an excess of goods and service exports over imports) was the only way a nation could gain from trade. This same idea is expressed by modern-day patriots who reason, "If I buy a Sony laptop computer from Japan, I have the laptop and Japan has the money. On the other hand, if I buy a Dell laptop in the United States, I have the laptop and the United States has the money. I should therefore 'buy American.'" This sort of reasoning leads to the conclusion that the persistent international **trade deficit** that the United States experiences year after year is bad for America. Let's see if this conclusion makes any sense.

MODERN-DAY MERCANTILISTS

During any given month, you cannot fail to see headlines about our continuing (or growing) trade deficit. Even if you are not quite sure how to calculate our international trade deficit, you might guess that the problem seems to be that we are importing more than we are exporting.

To understand the actual numbers reported in the press, you must understand that there are several components of trade deficits. The most

Table 27–1 Exports and Imports of Goods (billions of dollars)

Year	Exports	Imports	Deficit
1998	670.4	−917.1	−246.7
1999	684.0	−1,030.0	−346.0
2000	772.0	−1,224.4	−452.4
2001	718.7	−1,145.9	−427.2
2002	682.4	−1,164.7	−482.3
2003	713.4	−1,260.7	−547.3
2004	807.5	−1,472.9	−665.4
2005	894.6	−1,677.4	−782.8
2006	1,023.1	−1,861.4	−838.3
2007	1,148.5	−1,967.9	−819.4
2008	1,327.7	−2,182.0	−854.3

Source: U.S. Department of Commerce, Bureau of Economic Analysis.
Note: Sums may not add to totals due to rounding. Figures for 2008 are preliminary estimates.

obvious part consists of merchandise exports and imports. This is the number that receives the most coverage in the press. Table 27–1 shows the merchandise (goods) trade deficit for the United States for a recent ten-year period.

It looks pretty bad, doesn't it? It seems as if we've become addicted to imports! But merchandise is not the only thing that we buy and sell abroad. Increasingly, service exports and imports account for a major aspect of international trade, at least in the United States. (Some of the types of services we export involve accounting, legal research, **investment** advice, travel and transportation, and medical research.) For these and other service items, even mercantilists would be happy to know that the United States consistently exports more than it imports, as you can see in Table 27–2 on the next page, which shows the *net* balance of trade for the various categories of services.

The Link between Imports and Exports

Obviously, a comparison of the two tables still shows a substantial trade deficit, no matter how many times you look at the numbers. Should residents of the United States be worried? Before we can answer this question, we must look at some basic propositions about the relationship between imports and exports.

We begin by considering how we pay for the foreign goods and services that we import. Countries do not ship goods to the United States

Table 27–2 Net Exports of Services (billions of dollars)

Year	Net Service Exports
1998	82.1
1999	82.7
2000	74.9
2001	64.4
2002	61.2
2003	52.4
2004	54.1
2005	66.0
2006	85.0
2007	119.1
2008	145.2

Source: U.S. Department of Commerce, Bureau of Economic Analysis.
Note: Figures for 2008 are preliminary estimates.

simply to hold pieces of paper in exchange. Businesses in the rest of the world ship us goods and services because they want goods and services in exchange. That means only one thing, then: *In the long run, we pay for imports with exports. So in the long run, imports must equal exports.* The short run is a different story, of course. Imports can be paid for by the sale of real and financial **assets,** such as land, **shares of stock,** and **bonds,** or through an extension of credit from other countries. But in the long run, foreigners eventually want goods and services in return for the goods and services they send us. **Consumption** is, after all, the ultimate objective of production.

Because imports are paid for with exports in the long run, any attempt to reduce this country's trade deficit by restricting imports must also affect exports. In fact, a direct corollary of our first proposition must be that *any restrictions on imports must ultimately lead to a reduction in exports.* Thus every time politicians call for a reduction in our trade deficit, they are implicitly calling for a reduction in exports, at least in the long run.

It is possible that politicians don't understand this, but even if they did, they might still call for restricting imports. After all, it is easy for the domestic firms that lose business to foreign competition to claim that every dollar of imports represents a lost dollar of sales for them—implying, of course, a corresponding reduction in U.S. employment. In contrast, the tens of thousands of exporters of U.S. goods and services probably won't ever be able to put an exact value on their reduced sales and employment due to proposed and actual import restrictions. Hence the people with "evidence" about the supposed harms of imports will always outnumber those businesses who lose export sales when international trade is restricted.

A Renegade View of Imports?

Many discussions about international trade have to do with the supposed "unfairness" of imports. Somehow, it is argued, when goods come in from a foreign land, the result is unfair to the firms and workers who must compete with those imports. To see how such reasoning is no reasoning at all, one need only consider a simple example.

Assume that you have just discovered a way to produce textiles at one-tenth the cost of your closest competitors, who are located in South Carolina. You set up your base of operations in Florida and start selling your textiles at lower prices than your South Carolina competitors do. Your workers are appreciative of their jobs, and your **shareholders** are appreciative of their profits. To be sure, the textile owners and employees in South Carolina may not be happy, but there is nothing legally they can do about it. This, of course, is the essence of unfettered trade among the fifty states: Production takes place where costs are lowest and consumers benefit from the lower prices that result.

Now let's assume that you build the same facility in Florida, but instead of actually producing the textiles yourself, you secretly have them brought from South Africa to sell, as before, at lower prices than those at which the South Carolina firms can profitably produce. If everyone continues to believe that you are producing the textiles on your own, there will be no problems. But if anybody finds out that you are importing the textiles, the political wrath of members of Congress from South Carolina will descend on you. They will try to prohibit the importation of "cheap" textiles from South Africa or put a high tax, or **tariff,** on those textiles.

Is there really any difference between these two "production processes"? The first one involves the use of some textile machinery within the United States, while the second involves having a ship and some trucks pick up the textiles and drop them off at the "factory" in Florida. Are they really any different? We think not. Such is the conclusion when using positive economic analysis. Once the world of politics gets involved, however, the domestic production process is favored and the production process that involves imports is frowned upon.

The Other Side of Trade Deficits

Most discussions of the trade deficit are further flawed by the fact that they completely ignore the mirror image of the deficit. In the short run, when exports of goods and services don't match up, dollar for dollar, with imports, the trading partners involved must obviously make arrangements for short-run methods to pay for the difference. For example, when the United States is importing more goods and services than it is exporting, we must be selling real and financial assets to our trading partners.

For example, we might be borrowing from abroad (selling bonds) or selling shares of stock in U.S. corporations. (In the late 1990s, we also sold real estate, such as golf courses and office buildings.)

Now, at first blush, this sounds like we are "mortgaging the future," selling assets and borrowing funds in order to consume more now. But there is a different way to look at this: America is the safest, most productive place in the world to invest. *If the rest of the world is to be able to invest in the United States, we must run a trade deficit.* This proposition is a simple matter of arithmetic.

When, say, a South Korean automobile company builds a factory in the United States, there is an inflow of funds from South Korea to the United States. When foreign residents buy U.S. government securities, there is an inflow of funds from other countries to the United States. These investments are usually called *private capital flows,* and they include private land purchases, acquisitions of corporate stock shares, and purchases of government bonds. Virtually every year for at least thirty years, foreign residents have invested more in the United States than U.S. residents have invested abroad. This net inflow of capital funds from abroad is called a **capital account surplus.**

As a glance at Figure 27–1 reveals, this net inflow of investment funds into the United States nearly mirrors the trade deficit that the

Figure 27–1 The Relationship between the Current Account and the Capital Account

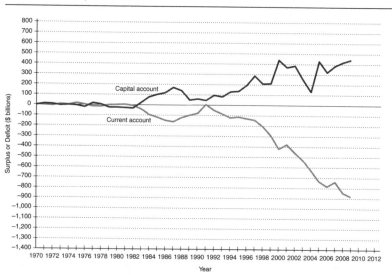

Sources: International Monetary Fund; *Economic Indicators.*

United States experiences each year. That is, when the current account trade deficit is small, the capital account surplus is small, and when the current account deficit is large, so is the capital account surplus. Is this just a coincidence? Certainly not. Think about it. If a foreign resident wants to buy stock in a U.S. company, that foreign resident must obtain dollars to pay for the stock. While it is true that the foreign resident simply goes to the foreign exchange market to do so, these dollars must somehow get supplied to the foreign exchange market. That supply of dollars must in turn come from the excess of U.S. goods and services imports over exports each year. In other words, *our international trade deficit supplies the dollars in foreign exchange markets necessary for foreigners to invest in the United States.* If Americans did not import more goods and services than they export, foreign residents could not invest in the United States.

THE SWEEP OF HISTORY

Contrary to what you might think from reading the newspapers, although the United States has been running a trade deficit for the past twenty-five years, this is not the first time we have run such a deficit over a long period of time. Indeed, from the Civil War until World War I, the United States ran a trade deficit year after year, borrowing funds and selling corporate stock all around the world. Were the consequences disastrous? Hardly. We used the funds we obtained from abroad to build railroads and steel mills and much of the rest of our industrial base, as well as to settle the West. We benefited from having access to low-cost finance (which we used to purchase key goods from abroad), and foreigners benefited from risk-adjusted rates of return that were higher than they could obtain in their home countries.

Beginning in World War I, this pattern reversed itself. Americans began lending money to Europeans to help them finance their war expenditures and then after the war lent them funds to rebuild. This pattern of American lending abroad continued through World War II and on until the early 1980s. All the while, we were running a trade surplus, exporting more goods and services than we were importing. Foreign residents were financing their purchases from us by borrowing and by selling us shares of stock in their corporations. They benefited by getting access to lower-cost finance and goods than they otherwise could have obtained. We benefited by selling our goods at a better price than we could get at home and also by earning a higher net rate of return than we could have obtained if we had invested only in domestic assets.

You can now see that the trade deficits of recent decades are a return to the pattern of the late nineteenth and early twentieth centuries. The

United States is once again the nation offering the highest risk-adjusted return, so foreigners invest here. There is one key difference between now and one hundred years ago, however. Back then, virtually all of the borrowing was being done by the private sector, so one could be reasonably certain that it was going to turn out to yield net benefits. Today, much of the borrowing is being done by the U.S. government. Will this turn out to yield net benefits? Only time will tell.

FOR CRITICAL ANALYSIS

1. Why can't competing producers in different states prevent "imports" into their own state? (*Hint:* To what document written over two hundred years ago are the states still subject?)

2. How does the concept of "buy local" relate to concerns about trade deficits on an international basis?

3. Does it matter to you where the product you are buying has been manufactured? Why or why not?

CHAPTER 28

The Value of the Dollar

When the euro was introduced in 1999, you could purchase one for $1.18. Three years later, when euro banknotes and coins began circulating as the monetary unit of most of the **European Union (EU),** the market price of the euro had fallen to $0.90. Since then, the euro's price has fluctuated between $0.86 and $1.60. This pattern of fluctuating prices is not unique to the euro. In a world of **flexible exchange rates,** the prices at which different **currencies** trade for each other is determined by the forces of world **demand** and **supply.** Thus if the demand for euros rises, its price will rise, and if its demand falls, so too will its price. And what is true for the euro is just as true for the British pound sterling, the Japanese yen, and our very own U.S. dollar. As we shall see, these changes in market forces, and the resulting changes in **exchange rates,** play a key role in determining patterns of international trade.

SOME TERMINOLOGY

Although we referred to the dollar price of the euro, we could just as well have talked of the euro price of the dollar. Thus if it takes $1.25 to purchase a euro, it must also be true that a dollar buys less than a euro. In fact, it buys exactly 1/1.25 euros in this example. That is, the euro price of the dollar is €0.80 (where € is the symbol for the euro). The exchange rate between the two currencies can be expressed either way, although in America people usually refer to the exchange rate as the dollar price of foreign currency, and so too shall we. In this example, the exchange rate between the dollar and the euro is thus $1.25.

You will also hear some people, especially journalists and politicians, talk about a "stronger" or "weaker" dollar, accompanied by pronouncements that one or the other condition is good for America. When people say the dollar has gotten "stronger," what they mean is that one dollar will buy more units of foreign currency than it used to. Hence a reduction in the exchange rate from, say, $1.25 to $1.20 per euro amounts to a stronger dollar. Conversely, if the dollar price of the euro rises from $1.25 to $1.35, this would mean that the dollar was weaker, because one dollar would buy fewer euros.

GOOD NEWS OR BAD?

Is a weaker dollar good news or bad? Like most value judgments (notice the words *good* and *bad*), the answer is in the eye of the beholder. Suppose the price of the euro rises from $1.25 to $1.50. We say that the dollar has gotten weaker relative to the euro because people must pay more dollars for each euro. Because American consumers must eventually come up with euros if they want to buy French wine or Italian pasta, when the euro becomes more expensive, European goods become more expensive for American consumers.[1] So from the perspective of American consumers, a weak dollar is bad news.

But producers in America may have a different view of the world. For example, automobile manufacturers with plants in America compete with manufacturers that have European facilities. When the dollar price of the euro rises, so does the dollar price of cars made in Europe. This induces some American consumers to "buy American," which is surely good news for the companies that receive their business. Similarly, recall that the *rise* in the price of the euro is equivalent to a *fall* in the price of the dollar. Such a move in the exchange rate makes American-made goods cheaper abroad. As a result, foreign consumers are also more likely to "buy American," again good news for the companies from whom they purchase. Thus a weaker dollar encourages exports and discourages imports, but whether that is "good" or "bad" news is clearly a matter on which people might reasonably disagree.

Now, what about the consequences of a "stronger" dollar? When the dollar can buy more euros, this means it can also buy more European goods. This clearly benefits American consumers, so we conclude that they like a strong dollar. American producers, however, will have a different take on matters. They will lose business from American customers, who are now more likely to "buy European." In addition, people in the

---

1. Of course, consumers typically don't physically obtain the euros themselves, but the importers who bring the goods in on their behalf must certainly do so.

EU will now find American goods more expensive because the dollar is now more expensive. So they will buy fewer American goods and make more purchases at home. Thus we conclude that a stronger dollar will encourage imports into America and discourage exports from America. Presumably, American consumers and producers will have much different opinions on whether this is good news or bad.

PURCHASING POWER PARITY

Of course, exchange rates don't just move around without cause. There are four well-established forces that play key roles in making them what they are. The first of these, which is by far the most important long-run determinant of exchange rates, is called **purchasing power parity (PPP)**. This principle simply states that the relative values of different currencies must ultimately reflect their **purchasing power** in their home countries.

To see how this works, let's consider the United States and Switzerland, which uses the Swiss franc as its currency. Over the past fifty years, the exchange rate between these two currencies has varied between roughly $0.25 and $1.00, that is, by a factor of 4. In the 1960s, for example, the exchange rate was near the bottom end of that range, but it has followed a persistent rise until quite recently, albeit with some ups and downs along the way. The reason the Swiss franc rose in value relative to the U.S. dollar is simple: Typically, the **inflation** rate in Switzerland has been much lower than in the United States. The amount of goods that American dollars would buy generally has been shrinking, so the Swiss demand for dollars has fallen, even as Americans have tried to unload their depreciating dollars for Swiss francs. Together these forces helped push the value of the Swiss franc up, and so the exchange rate rose, to $0.40, then $0.70, and even briefly to just about $1.00, before it dropped back into the neighborhood of $0.70.

This process applies across all countries. When the **price level** rises in country A relative to the price level in country B, people in both nations will switch some of their purchases of goods from country A to country B. This will push down the value of A's currency and push up the value of B's currency. In fact, this tendency is so strong that it will continue until "parity" is reached. If A's price level *rises* 20 percent relative to B's price level, then A's currency ultimately will *fall* in value by 20 percent relative to B's currency. It may take a while for this adjustment to work out, and it may be temporarily masked by some of the forces we shall talk about next, but eventually it will happen.

INTEREST RATES

One key reason for wishing to acquire the currency of another nation is that you want to acquire goods produced in that nation. But there is another reason: You may wish to invest or to lend funds in that nation. For example, suppose you wanted to purchase **bonds** issued by a Canadian corporation. These would be denominated in Canadian dollars (C$), so you would first have to obtain those Canadian dollars before you could purchase the bonds. Given this, it should be apparent that one of the factors influencing your demand for Canadian dollars is the *rate of return,* or interest rate, on **investments** in Canada, compared to the interest rate on investments elsewhere. The simplest way of putting this is that if interest rates in Canada rise relative to interest rates in the United States, investors will want to move funds from the United States into Canada. That is, there will be a drop in the demand for U.S. dollars and a rise in the demand for Canadian dollars, and so the exchange rate will rise— you will have to give up more U.S. dollars to obtain one Canadian dollar. The U.S. dollar will have become "weaker" against the Canadian currency.

Note that the interest rates of which we speak are **real interest rates,** that is, adjusted for any expected inflation. If interest rates rise in Canada because of an increase in the expected inflation rate there, this hardly makes them more attractive to American or European or Chinese investors. It simply neutralizes the effects of the higher expected inflation. Similarly, we must be careful to compare interest rates on obligations that have the same **default risk.** If the interest rate is high on bonds issued by a Canadian company that is in danger of **bankruptcy,** that higher interest rate simply compensates **bondholders** for the added default risk they face; it doesn't make those bonds unusually attractive to investors in the United States or elsewhere.

But as long as we are careful to adjust for expected inflation and risk, interest rate differentials can sometimes be quite useful in understanding events. For example, during the late nineteenth century, inflation- and risk-adjusted interest rates were higher in the United States than they were in Britain because America was rebuilding from the Civil War, settling the West, and industrializing at a rapid rate. All of these factors made America a productive place in which to invest. The higher rate of return in America made it attractive for British investors to lend funds to American firms, which in turn meant a higher demand for American dollars. As a result, the American dollar was more valuable on world markets than it otherwise would have been.

HARD CURRENCY

If you've ever visited a developing nation or a formerly Communist country, you may have heard people refer to "hard currency." You may even have had them insist you pay for your purchases not with the local currency but with American dollars or euros or even Swiss francs. The reasoning behind this insistence is simple.

In such countries, whatever the *current* state of economic and political affairs, the *future* state of both is often filled with great uncertainty. Perhaps the current government's political support is not too secure. Or there may be the simmering threat of a military-backed coup. Or maybe there is a suspicion that the national government won't be able to finance its future spending with conventional taxes. Should any of these eventualities be realized, the likely result is that the government will resort to printing money as a means of financing its activities, causing future high inflation that will devastate the purchasing power of the local currency. And because the exact timing and magnitude of this outcome are highly uncertain, so is the expected future value of the local currency.

To reduce their risk, people thus try to hold currencies whose value is unlikely to be subject to political vagaries—and these are currencies issued by strong democratic governments, such as those in the United States and the EU. This increases the demand for such currencies and thus tends to set their values in world markets higher than they otherwise would be. The reference to "hard currency" stems from the notion that the purchasing power of such currencies is as stable as a rock—which it is, compared to the local monies that people are trying to avoid holding.

BOEING AND THE BEATLES

The final key factor that helps determine exchange rates is quite simply the relative attractiveness of the goods produced in various nations. Consider the Boeing Corporation, long regarded as the maker of some of the best commercial jet planes in existence. Airlines all over the world purchase billions of dollars' worth of Boeing aircraft every year. To do this, they must acquire U.S. dollars, and their demand for dollars makes the value of the dollar on world markets higher than it otherwise would be.

Of course, the residents of foreign countries have been known to produce some nice products themselves. Many people feel that the best wines come from France, the best ties from Italy, and so forth. And then there are the Beatles, perhaps the most prolific and popular rock group ever, at least measured by worldwide sales of music. When the Beatles hit the music scene in the 1960s, millions of Americans wanted to acquire recordings of their songs. To do so, they first had to acquire pounds sterling (the money used in Britain). This increased the demand for pounds sterling and thus caused the dollar price of the pound to rise in foreign exchange markets. So the next time you are paying to download music of the British rock group Coldplay, you will know that your decision to buy their music has pushed the dollar price of the pound sterling up, even if just by the tiniest of amounts.

FOR CRITICAL ANALYSIS

1. Although the United Kingdom is a member of the EU, it does not use the euro as its monetary unit. Instead it uses the pound sterling. If the U.K. decided to switch from the pound to the euro, how might this decision affect the value of the euro in foreign exchange markets?

2. In an effort to discourage drug smugglers from using U.S. currency in major drug deals, the U.S. government refuses to issue currency in denominations greater than $100. How does this policy decision affect the demand for dollars and thus the exchange rate between the dollar and other currencies, such as the euro (which comes in denominations as big as €500)?

3. Sometimes national governments decide that they don't want their currencies to be any lower in value than they currently are. Explain how, if a country wants to raise the value of its currency in foreign exchange markets, it might use the following tools to do so:

   (a) Altering the rate of growth in its money supply, thus changing the current and expected inflation rate
   (b) Limiting the ability of citizens to invest in foreign nations
   (c) Imposing **tariffs** or **quotas** on imports
   (d) Subsidizing exports by domestic firms

GLOSSARY

abject poverty: surviving on the equivalent of $1 or less of income per person per day

adjustable-rate mortgage (ARM): debt used to finance house purchases, the interest rate on which changes depending on current market conditions

adverse selection: a process in which "undesirable" (high-cost or high-risk) participants tend to dominate one side of a market, causing adverse effects for the other side; often results from *asymmetric information*

aggregate demand: the total value of all planned spending on goods and services by all economic entities in the economy

appropriations bills: legislation that determines the size of government discretionary spending

asset: any valuable good capable of yielding flows of income or services over time

asset-backed security (ABS): a bond that has other assets (such as home mortgages) as collateral

asymmetric information: a circumstance in which participants on one side of a market have more information than participants on the other side of the market; often results in adverse selection

average tax rate: total taxes divided by income

balance sheet: a written record of assets and liabilities

bank run: an attempt by many of a bank's depositors to convert checkable and savings deposits into currency because of a perceived fear for the bank's solvency

bankruptcy: a state of being legally declared unable to pay one's debts so that some or all of the indebtedness is legally wiped out by the courts

bond: a debt conferring the right to receive a specific series of money payments in the future

bondholders: the owners of government or corporate bonds

book value: asset valuations that are based on the original purchase price of the assets rather than current market values

bubble: an episode in which asset prices exceed their values based on economic fundamentals, as determined by real future profits or service flows

budget constraint: all of the possible combinations of goods that can be purchased at given prices and given income

budget deficit: the excess of government spending over government revenues during a given time period

business cycles: the ups and downs in overall business activity, evidenced by changes in GDP, employment, and the price level

capital account surplus: a net inflow of capital funds (loans and investments) into a nation

capital ratio: the value of assets divided by the value of debt

capital stock: the collection of productive assets that can be combined with other inputs, such as labor, to produce goods and services

cash flow: cash receipts minus cash payments

central bank: a banker's bank, usually a government institution that also serves as the country's treasury's bank; central banks normally regulate commercial banks

checkable deposits: accounts at depository institutions that are payable on demand, either by means of a check or by direct withdrawal, as through an automated teller machine (ATM)

civil law system: a legal system in which statutes passed by legislatures and executive decrees, rather than judicial decisions based on precedent, form the basis for most legal rules

collateral: assets that are forfeited in the event of default on a obligation

collateralized debt obligation (CDO): an obligation to pay that is guaranteed by the pledge of another asset

commercial bank: a financial institution that accepts demand deposits and makes loans and provides other financial services to the public

common law system: a legal system in which judicial decisions based on precedent, rather than executive decrees or statutes passed by legislatures, form the basis for most legal rules

comparative advantage: the ability to produce a good or service at a lower opportunity cost compared to other producers

constant-quality price: price adjusted for any change in the quality of the good or service

consumer price index (CPI): a measure of the dollar cost of purchasing a bundle of goods and services assumed to be representative of the consumption pattern of a typical consumer; one measure of the price level

consumption: spending by consumers on new goods and services

core inflation: a measure of the overall rate of change in prices of goods, excluding energy and food

cost of living: the dollar cost (relative to a base year) of achieving a given level of satisfaction

credit-default swap: a financial contract in which the buyer of the swap makes a series of payments to the seller, who agrees to makes a payoff to the buyer if an underlying financial instrument (such as a bond) goes into default

creditor: an institution or individual that is owed money by another institution or individual

currency: paper money and coins issued by the government to serve as a medium of exchange

default: failure to meet obligations, for example, the failure to make debt payments

default risk: an estimation combining the probability that a contract will not be adhered to and the magnitude of the loss that will occur if it is not

deflation: a decline in the average level of the prices of goods and services

demand: the willingness and ability to purchase goods

depository institutions: financial institutions that accept deposits from savers and lend those deposits out to borrowers

depression: a severe recession

direct foreign investment: resources provided to individuals and firms in a nation by individuals or firms located in other countries, often taking the form of foreign subsidiary or branch operations of a parent company

disability payments: cash payments made to persons whose physical or mental disabilities prevent them from working

discouraged workers: persons who have dropped out of the labor force because they are unable to find suitable work

discretionary spending: government spending that is decided on anew each year, rather than being determined by a formula or set of rules

disposable income: income remaining after all taxes, retirement contributions, and the like are deducted

dividends: payments made by a corporation to owners of shares of its stock, generally based on the corporation's profits

drift: the average annual rate at which stock prices change over a long period of time

dumping: the sale of goods in a foreign country at a price below the market price charged for the same goods in the domestic market or at a price below the cost of production

dynamic economic analysis: a mode of analysis that recognizes that people respond to changes in incentives and that takes these responses into account when evaluating the effects of policies

earned income tax credit: a federal tax program that permits negative taxes, that is, that provides for payments to people (instead of collecting taxes from them) if their incomes go below a predetermined level

economic growth: sustained increases in real per capita income

elasticity: a measure of the responsiveness of one variable to a change in another variable

entitlement programs: government programs for which spending is determined chiefly by formulas or rules that specify who is eligible for funds and how much they may receive

equity: assets minus liabilities; net asset value

European Union (EU): a supranational entity resulting from an agreement among European nations to closely integrate the economic, political, and legal systems of the twenty-seven individual member nations

excess reserves: funds kept on hand by commercial banks to meet the transactions demands of customers and to serve as precautionary sources of funds in the event of a bank run; may be held as vault cash or as deposits at the Fed

exchange rate: the price of a currency expressed in terms of another currency

expansion: a period in which economic activity, measured by industrial production, employment, real income, and wholesale and retail sales, is growing on a sustained basis

expansive monetary policy: actions that tend to increase the level or rate of growth of the money supply

expected rate of inflation: the rate at which the average level of prices of goods and services is expected to rise

fair-value accounting: an accounting method in which the reported values of assets are adjusted to reflect (estimates of) the current market values of those assets rather than their purchase prices or their stated maturity value

federal budget deficit: the excess of the national government's spending over its receipts

federal funds rate: the nominal interest rate at which banks can borrow reserves from one another

Federal Reserve System (the Fed): the central bank of the United States

fiscal policy: discretionary changes in government spending or taxes that alter the overall state of the economy, including employment, investment, and output

fiscal year: the accounting year used by a government or business; for the federal government, the fiscal year runs from October 1 to September 30

flexible exchange rates: exchange rates that are free to move in response to market forces

foreclosure: the legal process by which a borrower in default under a mortgage is deprived of his or her interest in the mortgaged property

gains from trade: the extent to which individuals, firms, or nations benefit from engaging in voluntary exchange

globalization: the integration of national economies into an international economy

government-sponsored enterprise (GSE): a federally chartered corporation that is privately owned, designed to provide a source of credit nationwide, and limited to servicing one economic sector

gross domestic product (GDP): the dollar value of all new, domestically produced final goods and services in an economy

gross public debt: all public debt, including that owned by agencies of the government issuing it

hedge funds: investment companies that require large initial deposits by investors and pursue high-risk investments in the hope of achieving high returns

human capital: the productive capacity of human beings

illiquid: when used in reference to a company or person: having insufficient cash on hand to meet current liabilities; when used in reference to an asset: that which cannot be easily and cheaply converted into cash.

in-kind transfer: the provision of goods and services rather than cash, as in the case of Medicare, Medicaid, or subsidized housing

income mobility: the tendency of people to move around in the income distribution over time

Industrial Revolution: the widespread radical socioeconomic changes that took place in England and many other nations beginning in the late eighteenth century, brought about when extensive mechanization of production systems resulted in a shift from home-based hand manufacturing to large-scale factory production

inflation: a rise in the average level of the prices of goods and services

inflationary premium: the additional premium, in percent per year, that people are willing to pay to have dollars sooner rather than later simply because inflation is expected in the future

inflation tax: the decline in the real value or purchasing power of money balances due to inflation

inside information: valuable information about future economic performance that is not generally available to the public

insolvent: describing a financial condition in which the value of one's assets is less than the value of one's liabilities

insourcing: the use of domestic workers to perform a service traditionally done by foreign workers

institutions: the basic rules, customs, and practices of society

interagency borrowings: loans from one part of the federal government to another

interest group: a collection of individuals with common aims

intermediate goods: goods that contribute to present or future consumer welfare but are not direct sources of utility themselves; typically, they are used up in the production of final goods and services

investment: the creation of new machines, factories, and other assets that enable the production of more goods and services in the future

investment bank: a financial institution that helps companies or municipalities obtain financing by selling stocks or bonds on their behalf

investment security: a debt obligation for which the default risk is low

labor force: individuals aged sixteen and over who either have jobs or are looking and available for work

labor supply curve: a schedule showing the quantity of labor supplied at each wage rate

liabilities: amounts owed; the legal claims against an individual or against an institution by those who are not owners of that institution

loophole: a provision of the tax code that enables a narrow group of beneficiaries to achieve a lower effective tax rate

Luddites: followers of General Ned Ludd who early in the nineteenth century led destructive protests against mechanization in English textile mills; a term used today to refer to people who object to technological change

mandates: in the context of governments, regulations or laws that require other governments, private individuals, or firms to spend money to achieve goals specified by the government

marginal tax rate: the percentage of the last dollar earned that is paid in taxes

mark to market: an accounting practice in which the reported values of assets are adjusted to reflect (estimates of) the current market values of those assets rather than their purchase prices or their stated maturity value

median age: the age that separates the older half of the population from the younger half

median income: the income that separates the higher-income half of the population from the lower-income half

medium of exchange: any asset that sellers will generally accept as payment

mercantilists: believers in the doctrine of mercantilism, which asserted (among other things) that exports were the principal objective of international trade because they permitted the accumulation of gold

microeconomics: the study of decision making by consumers and by firms and of the market equilibria that result

monetary policy: the use of changes in the amount of money in circulation to affect interest rates, credit markets, inflation (or deflation), and unemployment

money supply: the sum of checkable deposits and currency in the hands of the public

moral hazard: the tendency of an entity insulated from risk to behave differently than it would behave if it were fully exposed to the risk

mortgage-backed security (MBS): a debt obligation that pledges home mortgages as collateral

mortgages: debts that are incurred to buy a house and provide that if the debt is not paid, the house can be sold by the creditor and the proceeds used to pay that debt

mutual funds: a pool of money that is invested in assets, often shares of stock in corporations

natural-resource endowments: the collection of naturally occurring minerals (such as oil and iron ore) and living things (such as forests and fish stocks) that can be used to produce goods and services

negative tax: a payment from the government to an individual that is based on the individual's income

net public debt: the portion of the public debt that is owned outside of the government issuing it

net worth: the excess of assets over liabilities

nominal income: income expressed in terms of a monetary unit, such as the dollar

nominal interest rate: the premium, in percent per year, that people are willing to pay to have dollars sooner rather than later

nominal prices: the exchange value of goods, expressed in terms of a unit of account, such as the dollar or the euro

normal good: a good for which the demand increases as people's income or wealth grows

opportunity cost: the highest-valued, next-best alternative that must be sacrificed to obtain something

outsourcing: the use of labor in another country to perform service work traditionally done by domestic workers

pay-as-you-go system: a scheme in which current cash outflows are funded (paid for) with current cash inflows

payroll taxes: taxes that are levied on income specifically generated by workforce participation and that are generally earmarked for spending on specific programs, such as Social Security

per capita income: gross domestic product (GDP) divided by population

per capita real net public debt: net public debt, deflated by the price level and divided by the population

perfectly inelastic: having an elasticity (or responsiveness) of zero

permanent income: the sustained or average level of income that one expects will be observed over a long period of time

physical capital: the productive capacity of physical assets, such as buildings

price controls: government rules that limit the prices firms may charge for the goods or services they sell

price level: the average current-year cost, measured relative to the average base-year cost, of a typical basket of goods and services

productivity: output per unit of input

profits: the difference between revenue and cost

progressive tax system: a set of rules that result in the collection of a larger share of income as taxes when income rises

property and contract rights: legal rules governing the use and exchange of property and the enforceable agreements between people or businesses

proportional tax system: a set of rules that result in the collection of an unchanging share of income as income changes

protectionism: economic policy of promoting favored domestic industries through the use of high tariffs and quotas and other trade restrictions to reduce imports

protectionist: any attitude or policy that seeks to prevent foreigners from competing with domestic firms or individuals

public debt: the amount of money owed by a government to its creditors

purchasing power: a measure of the amount of goods and services that can be purchased with a given amount of money

purchasing power parity (PPP): the principle that the relative values of different currencies must reflect their purchasing power in their home countries

quota: a limit on the amount of a good that may be imported; generally used to reduce imports so as to protect the economic interests of domestic industries that compete with the imports

random walk: a pattern of price (or other) movements in which the best expectation of a future value is today's value and in which the variability of price (or other entity) is constant over time

real gross domestic product (real GDP): the inflation-adjusted level of new, domestically produced final goods and services

real income: income adjusted for inflation; equivalently, income expressed in terms of goods and services

real interest rate: the premium, in percent per year, that people are willing to pay to have goods sooner rather than later

real per capita income: GDP corrected for inflation and divided by the population—a measure of the amount of new domestic production of final goods and services per person

real price: price of a good or service adjusted for inflation; equivalently, the price of a good or service expressed in terms of other goods and services; see *relative prices*

real purchasing power: the amount of goods and services that can be acquired with an asset whose value is expressed in terms of the monetary unit of account (such as the dollar)

real tax rate: share of GDP controlled by the government

real wages: wages adjusted for changes in the price level

recession: a decline in the level of overall business activity

regressive tax system: a set of rules that result in the collection of a smaller share of income as taxes when income rises

relative prices: prices of goods and services compared to the prices of other goods and services; costs of goods and services measured in terms of other commodities

required reserves: funds that a commercial bank must lawfully maintain; they may be held in the form of vault cash or deposits at the Fed

reserves: assets held by depository institutions, typically in the form of currency held at the institution or as non-interest-bearing deposits held at the central bank, to meet customers' transaction needs and Fed legal requirements

resources: any items capable of satisfying individuals' desires or preferences or suitable for transformation into such goods

revealed preferences: consumers' tastes as demonstrated by the choices they make

rule of law: the principle that relations between individuals, businesses, and the government are governed by explicit rules that apply to everyone in society

saving: an addition to wealth, conventionally measured as disposable personal income minus consumption

savings: one's stock of wealth at a given moment in time

scarcity: a state of the world in which there are limited resources but unlimited demands, implying that we must make choices among alternatives

securitized: describing cash flow–producing assets pooled and repackaged into securities that are then sold to investors

shareholders: owners of shares of stock in a corporation

share of stock: claim to a specified portion of future net cash flows (or profits) of a corporation

solvent: describing a financial condition in which the value of one's assets is greater than the value of one's liabilities

standard of living: a summary measure of the level of per capita material welfare, often measured by per capita real GDP

static economic analysis: a mode of analysis that assumes for simplicity that people do not change their behavior when incentives change

stock: as applied to measurement, an amount measured at a particular moment in time

stockbroker: a middleman who sells shares of stock to individuals

subprime mortages: *mortgages* that entail the higher risk of loss for the lender

subsidies: government payments for the production of specific goods, generally intended to raise the profits of the firms producing those goods

supply: the willingness and ability to sell goods

tariff: a tax levied only on imports; generally used to reduce imports so as to protect the economic interests of domestic industries that compete with the imports

tax bracket: a range of income over which a specific marginal tax rate applies

tax credit: a direct reduction in tax liability, occasioned by a specific set of circumstances and not dependent on the taxpayer's tax bracket

tax evasion: the deliberate failure to pay taxes, usually by making a false report

tax rate: the percentage of a dollar of income that must be paid in taxes

tax rebate: a return of some previously paid taxes

trade barrier: a legal rule imposed by a nation that raises the costs of foreign firms seeking to sell goods in that nation; they include tariffs and quotas

trade deficit: an excess of the value of imports of goods and services over the value of the exports of goods and services

trade surplus: an excess of the value of exports of goods and services over the value of the imports of goods and services

underground economy: commercial transactions on which taxes and regulations are being avoided

unemployment rate: the number of persons looking and available for work, divided by the labor force

unfunded taxpayer liabilities: obligations of taxpayers for which no specific debt instruments have been issued

voucher: a written authorization, exchangeable for cash or services

wealth: the present value of all current and future income

wealth tax: a tax based on a person's net worth

World Trade Organization (WTO): an association of more than 150 nations that helps reduce trade barriers among its members and handles international trade disputes among them

write off: declare to be worthless

SELECTED REFERENCES
AND WEB LINKS

CHAPTER 1   Rich Nation, Poor Nation

Easterly, William, and Ross Levine. "Tropics, Germs, and Crops: How Endowments Influence Economic Development." *Journal of Monetary Economics* 50, no. 1 (2003): 3–39.

Mahoney, Paul G. "The Common Law and Economic Growth: Hayek Might Be Right." *Journal of Legal Studies* 30, no. 2 (2001): 503–525.

Rosenberg, Nathan, and L. E. Birdzell Jr. *How the West Grew Rich.* New York: Basic Books, 1987.

Spiers, Elizabeth. "The World's Worst Inflation." *Fortune*, August 18, 2008, p. 36.

www.worldbank.org. Official Web site of the World Bank.

CHAPTER 2   Return of the Luddites: Technophobia
             and Economic Growth

Evenson, R. E., and D. Gollin. "Assessing the Impact of the Green Revolution, 1960 to 2000." *Science,* May 2, 2003, pp. 758–762.

Lomborg, Bjorn. *The Skeptical Environmentalist: Measuring the Real State of the World.* Cambridge: Cambridge University Press, 2001.

Meiners, Roger E., and Andrew P. Morriss. "Property Rights and Pesticides." *PERC Policy Series (Bozeman)* 22 (2001).

Mokyr, Joel. *Lever of Riches: Technological Creativity and Economic Progress.* Oxford: Oxford University Press, 1990.

CHAPTER 3   The Lion, the Dragon, and the Tigers: Economic
             Growth in Asia

Hilsenrath, Jon E., and Rebecca Buckman. "Factory Employment Is Falling Worldwide." *Wall Street Journal*, October 20, 2003, p. A1.

"A Less Fiery Dragon?" *Economist*, December 1, 2007, p. 92.

Peerenboom, Randall. *China's Long March toward Rule of Law.* New York: Cambridge University Press, 2002.

Spence, Michael. "Why China Grows So Fast." *Wall Street Journal*, January 23, 2007.

Young, Alwyn. "Gold into Base Metals: Productivity Growth in the People's Republic of China during the Reform Period." *Journal of Political Economy* 3, no. 6 (2003): 1220–1262.

CHAPTER 4 Outsourcing and Economic Growth

Council of Economic Advisers. *Economic Report of the President.* Washington, D.C.: Government Printing Office, 2004.
Garten, Jeffrey E. "Offshoring: You Ain't Seen Nothin' Yet." *Business Week*, June 21, 2004, p. 28.
Gnuschke, John E., Jeff Wallace, Dennis R. Wilson, and Stephen C. Smith. "Outsourcing Production and Jobs: Costs and Benefits." *Business Perspectives* 16, no. 2 (2004): 12–18.
Irwin, Douglas A. "Free-Trade Worriers." *Wall Street Journal*, August 9, 2004, p. A12.

CHAPTER 5 Poverty, Capitalism, and Growth

Foundation for Teaching Economics. "Is Capitalism Good for the Poor?" (www.fte.org/capitalism/index.php)
Gwartney, James, Robert Lawson, and William Easterly. *Economic Freedom of the World: 2006 Annual Report.* Vancouver, Canada: Fraser Institute, 2006.
cia.gov/cia/publications/factbook. Central Intelligence Agency profiles of countries and territories.
www.freetheworld.com. Fraser Institute site on economic freedom around the world.

CHAPTER 6 Measuring GDP

"Grossly Distorted Picture." *Economist*, March 15, 2008, p. 92.
Steindel, Charles. "Chain Weighting: The New Approach to Measuring GDP." *Current Issues in Economics and Finance* 9, no. 1 (1995).
bea.gov/bea/dn/home/gdp.htm. GDP data from U.S. Department of Commerce, Bureau of Economic Analysis.

CHAPTER 7 What's in a Word? Plenty, When It's the "R" Word

Business Cycle Dating Committee. "The NBER's Recession Dating Procedure." National Bureau of Economic Research, 2003. (nber.org/cycles/recessions.html)
Conference Board. "Business Cycle Indicators." (www.globalindicators.org)

Layton, Allan P., and Anirvan Banerji. "What Is a Recession? A Reprise." *Applied Economics* 35, no. 16 (2003): 1789–1797.

www.bea.doc.gov. Web site of the U.S. Department of Commerce's Bureau of Economic Analysis.

CHAPTER 8 The Panic of '08

Friedman, Milton, and Anna J. Schwartz. *A Monetary History of the United States, 1867–1960.* Princeton, N.J: Princeton University Press, 1963.

Leonhardt, David. "Lesson from a Crisis: When Trust Vanishes, Worry." *New York Times*, October 1, 2008.

Nocera, Joe. "36 Hours of Alarm and Action as Crisis Spiraled." *New York Times*, October 2, 2008.

CHAPTER 9 The Case of the Disappearing Workers

Benjamin, Daniel K., and Kent G. P. Matthews. *U.S. and U.K. Unemployment between the Wars: A Doleful Story.* London: Institute for Economic Affairs, 1992.

Darby, Michael R. "Three-and-a-Half Million U.S. Employees Have Been Mislaid: Or, an Explanation of Unemployment, 1934–1941." *Journal of Political Economy* 84, no. 1 (1976): 1–16.

Wallis, John Joseph, and Daniel K. Benjamin. "Public Relief and Unemployment in the Great Depression." *Journal of Economic History* 41, no. 1 (1981): 97–102.

www.bls.gov. Web site of the U.S. Department of Labor's Bureau of Labor Statistics.

CHAPTER 10 Poverty, Wealth, and Equality

Becker, Gary S., and Richard A. Posner. "How to Make the Poor Poorer." *Wall Street Journal*, January 26, 2007, p. A11.

"Cheap and Cheerful." *Economist*, July 26, 2008, p. 90.

"Movin' On Up." *Wall Street Journal*, November 14, 2007.

U.S. Department of the Treasury. *Income Mobility in the U.S. from 1996 to 2005.* Washington, D.C.: Government Printing Office, 2007.

CHAPTER 11 Will It Be Inflation or Deflation?

Alchian, Armen A., and Reuben Kessel. "The Effects of Inflation." *Journal of Political Economy* 70, no. 6 (1962): 521–537.

Cagan, Phillip. "Monetary Dynamics of Hyperinflation." In *Studies in the Quantity Theory of Money*, ed. Milton Friedman. Chicago: University of Chicago Press, 1956.

Keynes, John Maynard. *The Economic Consequences of the Peace*. New York: Harcourt, Brace, 1920.

Spiers, Elizabeth. "The Great Inflation Cover-Up." *Fortune*, April 14, 2008, pp. 25–26.

CHAPTER 12   Is It Real, or Is It Nominal?

Bresnahan, Timothy F., and Robert J. Gordon (eds.). *The Economics of New Goods*. NBER Studies in Income and Wealth no. 58. Chicago: University of Chicago Press, 1997.

Goklany, Indur M., and Jerry Taylor. "A Big Surprise on Gas." *Los Angeles Times*, August 11, 2008.

www.bls.gov. Web site of the Bureau of Labor Statistics, U.S. Department of Labor.

www.eia.doe.gov. Web site of the Energy Information Administration, U.S. Department of Energy.

CHAPTER 13   The Growth of Big Government

Birnbaum, Jeffrey H. "The Return of Big Government: Federal Spending Is Skyrocketing, but Shockingly Little of It Is Related to Sept. 11." *Fortune*, September 16, 2002, p. 112.

"Can't Last: George Bush's Big-Government Conservatism." *Economist*, January 10, 2004, p. 23.

Peterson, Peter G. "Hear No Deficit, See No Deficit, Speak No Deficit." *Fortune*, August 23, 2004, p. 48.

Pierce, Vanessa. "Wasteful Spending Thwarts Recovery." *Insight on the News*, August 19, 2003, p. 28.

U.S. Office of Management and Budget. "Budget of the United States, Fiscal Year 2007." (www.whitehouse.gov/omb/budget)

CHAPTER 14   Debts and Deficits: What's a Trillion More or Less?

Barro, Robert J. "Are Government Bonds Net Wealth?" *Journal of Political Economy* 82, no. 6 (1974): 1095–1117.

Council of Economic Advisers. *Economic Report of the President*. Washington, D.C.: Government Printing Office, 2009.

The 2008 Annual Report of the Board of Trustees of the Federal Old-Age and Survivors Insurance and Federal Disability Insurance Trust Funds. Washington, D.C.: Government Printing Office, 2008.

CHAPTER 15 Higher Taxes Are in Your Future

Council of Economic Advisers. *Economic Report of the President.* Washington, D.C.: Government Printing Office, 2009.

Marquardt, Katy. "Maxing Out the National Debt Clock." *U.S. News & World Report,* October 9, 2008.

The 2008 Annual Report of the Board of Trustees of the Federal Old-Age and Survivors Insurance and Federal Disability Insurance Trust Funds. Washington, D.C.: Government Printing Office, 2008.

www.brillig.com/debt_clock. One of many private Web sites that track the U.S. national debt.

CHAPTER 16 Soak the Rich

Norton, Rob. "Corporate Taxation." *The Concise Encyclopedia of Economics.* (www.econlib.org/library/Enc/CorporateTaxation.html)

Rakowski, Eric. "Can Wealth Taxes Be Justified?" *Tax Law Review* 53, no. 3 (2000): 3–37.

Slemrod, Joel B. "Progressive Taxes." *The Concise Encyclopedia of Economics.* (www.econlib.org/library/Enc1/ProgressiveTaxes.html)

CHAPTER 17 The Myths of Social Security

Congressional Budget Office. "Social Security: A Primer." September 2001. (www.cbo.gov/showdoc.cfm?index=3213&sequence=0)

Engelhardt, Gary V., and Jonathan Gruber. *Social Security and the Evolution of Elderly Poverty.* NBER Working Paper no. 10466. Boston: National Bureau of Economic Research, 2004.

Oshio, Takashi. *Social Security and Trust Fund Management.* NBER Working Paper no. 10444. Boston: National Bureau of Economic Research, 2004.

www.ssa.gov. Web site of the Social Security Administration.

CHAPTER 18 The Hazards of High Taxes

Edwards, Chris. *Income Tax Rife with Complexity and Inefficiency.* Washington, D.C.: Cato Institute, 2006.

Goolsbee, Austan. "The Impact of the Corporate Income Tax: Evidence from State Organizational Form Data." *Journal of Public Economics* 88, no. 11 (2004): 2283–2299.

Harberger, Arnold C. "Three Basic Postulates for Applied Welfare Economics: An Interpretive Essay." *Journal of Economic Literature* 9, no. 3 (1971): 785–797.

Chapter 19 The Fed and Financial Panics

Friedman, Milton, and Anna J. Schwartz. *A Monetary History of the United States, 1867–1960*. Princeton, N.J.: Princeton University Press, 1963.

Goodman, Peter. "Taking a Hard New Look at a Greenspan Legacy." *New York Times*. October 9, 2008.

Norris, Floyd. "Plan B: Flood Banks with Cash." *New York Times*, October 10, 2008.

Chapter 20 Monetary Policy and Interest Rates

Demiralp, Selva, and Oscar Jorda. "The Response of Term Rates to Fed Announcements." *Journal of Money, Credit and Banking* 36, no. 3 (2004): 387–405.

Preiss, Michael. "Fighting the Federal Reserve Is a Losing Proposition." *Knight Ridder/Tribune Business News*, August 13, 2004.

Chapter 21 Credit Chaos

Calomiris, Charles W., and Peter J. Wallison. "Blame Fannie Mae and Congress for the Credit Mess." *Wall Street Journal*, September 23, 2008.

Duhigg, Charles. "Pressured to Take on Risk, Fannie Hit a Tipping Point." *New York Times*, October 5, 2008.

Leibowitz, Stan J. *Anatomy of a Train Wreck: Causes of the Mortgage Meltdown*. Oakland, Calif.: Independent Institute, 2008.

Chapter 22 Deposit Insurance and Financial Markets

Allen, Franklin, and Douglas Gale. "Competition and Financial Stability." *Journal of Money, Credit and Banking* 36, no. 3 (2004): S453–S480.

Bordo, M., H. Rockoff, and A. Redish. "The U.S. Banking System from a Northern Exposure: Stability versus Efficiency." *Journal of Economic History* 54, no. 2 (1994): 325–341.

Diamond, D., and P. Dybvig. "Bank Runs, Deposit Insurance, and Liquidity." *Journal of Political Economy* 91, no. 3 (1983): 401–419.

Friedman, Milton, and Anna J. Schwartz. *A Monetary History of the United States, 1867–1960*. Princeton, N.J.: Princeton University Press, 1963.

CHAPTER 23 How (Not) to Beat the Market

Chari, V. V., and Patrick J. Kehoe. "Hot Money." *Journal of Political Economy* 3, no. 6 (2003): 1262–1292.

Feinstone, Lauren J. "Minute by Minute: Efficiency, Normality, and Randomness in Intra-Daily Asset Prices." *Journal of Applied Econometrics* 2, no. 1 (1987): 193–214.

Malkiel, Burton G. *A Random Walk down Wall Street: Including a Life-Cycle Guide to Personal Investing.* New York: Norton, 1996.

Scheinkman, Jose A., and Wei Xiong. "Overconfidence and Speculative Bubbles." *Journal of Political Economy* 3, no. 6 (2003): 1183–1219.

CHAPTER 24 Credit-Card Crunch

Board of Governors of the Federal Reserve System. *Highlights of Final Rules regarding Credit Card Accounts.* December 18, 2008. (www .federalreserve.gov/newsevents/press/bcreg20081218a1.pdf)

Kaper, Stacy. "Fed Plans to Restrict Card-Rate Increase." *American Banker*, April 29, 2008.

Prater, Connie. "What the New Credit Card Reforms Mean for You." CreditCards.com, 2009. (www.creditcards.com/credit-card-news/what-the-new-credit-card-rules-mean-1282.php)

CHAPTER 25 The Opposition to Globalization

Frankel, J. A., and D. Romer. "Does Trade Cause Growth?" *American Economic Review* 89, no. 3 (1999): 379–399.

"Indian Call Center Lands in Ohio." *Fortune*, August 6, 2007, p. 23.

Makki, Shiva S., and Agapi Somwaru. "Impact of Foreign Direct Investment and Trade on Economic Growth: Evidence from Developing Countries." *American Journal of Agricultural Economics* 86, no. 3 (2004): 795–801.

CHAPTER 26 The $750,000 Job

Congressional Budget Office. "The Pros and Cons of Pursuing Free-Trade Agreements." July 2003. (www.cbo.gov/showdoc.cfm?index =4458&sequence=0)

Greider, William. "A New Giant Sucking Sound: China Is Taking Away Mexico's Jobs as Globalization Enters a Fateful New Stage." *Nation,* December 31, 2001, p. 22.

"Stolen Jobs? Offshoring." *Economist,* December 13, 2003, p. 15.

CHAPTER 27 The Trade Deficit

Congressional Budget Office. "Causes and Consequences of the Trade Deficit: An Overview." March 2000. (www.cbo.gov/showdoc .cfm?index=1897&sequence=0)

Congressional Budget Office. "The Decline in the U.S. Current-Account Balance since 1991." August 2004. (www.cbo.gov/showdoc .cfm?index=5722&sequence=0)

Cooper, James C., and Kathleen Madigan. "The Trade Deficit May Soon Cause Less Pain: A Weaker Dollar and Stronger Global Demand Will Slow Down the Beast." *Business Week,* July 26, 2004, p. 27.

CHAPTER 28 The Value of the Dollar

Clark, Peter, et al. *Exchange Rates and Economic Fundamentals.* IMF Occasional Paper no. 115. Washington, D.C.: International Monetary Fund, 1994.

Grant, James. "Is the Medicine Worse than the Illness?" *Wall Street Journal,* December 20, 2008.

finance.yahoo.com/currency-converter?u. One of many private currency converters available online.

www.exchange-rates.org. One of many private currency converters available online.

INDEX